Glimp

of New Zealand

by Gail Lawther

TEAMWORK
CRAFTBOOKS

CONTENTS

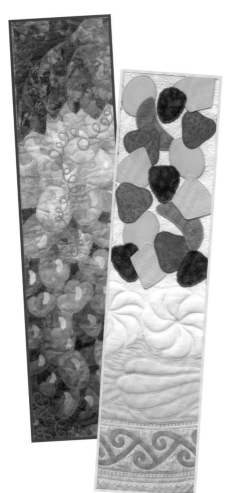

INTRODUCTION

Awesome!

My husband Chris and I have been lucky enough to visit New Zealand twice, and that's a word we heard a great deal when we were there. And with good reason; New Zealand is a spectacularly beautiful country, full of grand vistas – beaches, mountains, waterfalls, native bush, rivers, fertile plains. When we first told people that we were going, we had two reactions. People who'd been there themselves said 'Oh, you'll love New Zealand!' And people who hadn't said 'I'm so jealous: tell me all about it when you get back.' It's the only time that people have begged to see our holiday photographs!

We first went to New Zealand for a month over Christmas and New Year 2004/2005, as a belated 25th wedding anniversary present to ourselves, and we were bowled over by the country. We'd assumed originally that this would be a 'once-in-a-lifetime' trip, but we enjoyed our time there so much we couldn't wait to return. Three years later we had our chance, and returned for another month to revisit some of our favourite places and to explore some new ones. During our visits we've come to love New Zealand, but with only two months' experience, we can't truly say that we know it – it's been more like glimpses through a half-open door. We've had a chance to

Top to bottom: one of my classes at the Auckland Quilt Symposium 2005; boardwalk at Ahuriri Estuary, Napier; a traditional tram house in Thames (so called because they are built around original tram coaches); sleepy seal on a beach near Dunedin

peek at lots of different aspects of Kiwi life, culture, art, landscape, fauna and flora etc, each one leaving us wanting to see and know more. And of course like all travellers we've taken our photographs – literal snapshots that capture particular times and places.

On our first trip I had the chance to teach at the Auckland Quilt Symposium and in Dunedin, and to see some of the marvellous work being done by NZ quilters. On the second trip I taught at the Quilters' Barn in Blenheim (and bought lots of bits of New Zealand fabric, many of which I've incorporated into these quilts). Our visits seemed inseparable from quilting, and not surprisingly I came back from New Zealand with my head full of inspiration and ideas, but barely knew where to start. I did several quite large pieces inspired by different aspects of the country, but still had dozens more ideas I wanted to interpret in fabric. One day the perfect inspiration came: I would do a series of long, thin quilts. Each one would be like that view through a half-open door, giving the viewer a peep into the life, culture, history or decorative motifs of Aotearoa, the Land of the Long White Cloud. *Glimpses of New Zealand* was born.

While we were putting this book together I found my original notes to myself for the series of quilts: I had written '*could I do 12?!*' Could I do 12 indeed: as soon as I began working on them I had mentally designed 20, then it became 25,

Above: long white cloud over island off Auckland
Below: view from the so-called Centre of New Zealand, just outside Nelson

then 30; I finally called a halt at 35, working on the principle that if I did any more I wouldn't be able to carry them all at once to talks and shows. The quilts are all the same format, measuring roughly 40 x 10in, which gives them a visual unity, but each one has a different inspiration, and each one uses a different combination of quilting techniques. These techniques vary from the traditional (Log Cabin and other blocks, wholecloth and Hawaiian quilting), through more modern ones (machine quilting and appliqué, big-stitch quilting, fabric painting, beading) to the experimental (burning, fabric manipulation, printing on fabric, foiling).

The first section of the book features all the quilts, with the stories behind their inspiration and details of the materials and techniques used; we've also used the opportunity to include loads of our favourite photographs of New Zealand. Some of the photographs were direct or indirect inspiration for the quilts; others are just there because we like them, and think you will too. On these pages you'll also find lots of tips and techniques that I've used on the quilts which you may find useful for your own work. And if you fancy producing your own versions of some of my *Glimpses* quilts, the final part of the book gives patterns and instructions for around half the main quilts, along with more technical tips.

We hope you have a lot of fun reading these pages; we've tried to include all kinds of interesting bits and pieces, including the occasional Maori word or the odd intriguing fact. If you've been to New Zealand I hope it brings back lots of good memories; if you haven't been – what are you waiting for?! (I think I'm making the entire New Zealand Tourist Board redundant: I can do their work single-handed …) And, as I write this book, I've just been invited to join the teaching team for the wonderfully-named Remarkable Symposium in Queenstown in 2011. So, maybe there will be more *Glimpses of New Zealand* to come … watch this space!

Find out more …

If you'd like to know more about different aspects of New Zealand (I definitely ought to be on a retainer from the NZ tourist board …), there are numerous websites, books etc which will tell you about all kinds of things. Listed below are a few general ones, and after the details of each quilt we've also included ideas for more exploration related to that particular subject.

DK *Eyewitness Travel Guide* to New Zealand, published by Dorling Kindersley ISBN 9781405321051

Insight Guide to New Zealand, by Francis Dorai, ISBN 9789812586667

AA Spiral Guide to New Zealand, ISBN 9780749553661

Ultimate Experiences New Zealand, published by Rough Guides ISBN 9781843538257

www.newzealand.com – website for Tourism New Zealand

www.centralart.co.nz – a Queenstown gallery which provides a showcase for contemporary NZ artists

Top to bottom: Split Apple Rock, off the shore of the Abel Tasman National Park; one of many exotic blooms we saw on our travels; a typical Art Deco building in Napier

NEW ZEALAND

I've made my opening quilt a sampler of images and fabrics from the land of the kiwi

Bush walk through the Abel Tasman National Park

So many factors combine to create the modern country of New Zealand: Maori crafts, paua shell, kiwis, kauri wood, pukekos, the haka, sheep, Scottish influence, feijoa juice, possums, the call of the tui. To open this series of quilts I wanted to use the name of the country, and to capture some of these elements within the lettering – like a kind of New Zealand sampler. Many of the fabrics are homegrown Kiwi ones, and I've found others from my stash to complement them. I used double-sided bonding web to secure the letters on the backgrounds, then went round them all – and the background squares – with machine satin stitch (see below). I wanted to arrange the letters in a more interesting shape than simply piling them on top of each other, so I decided to stagger them down the gentle double-curved background. Working from the top, the different aspects I've celebrated on this quilt are:

N: Maori art, exemplified by various spirals and curved shapes in natural colours, offset by a batik foliage print.

E: Ferns and spirals, motifs seen everywhere in New Zealand art and design.

W: The scarlet blossoms of the pohutukawa tree, providing a perfect complement to a traditional red, black and white Maori pattern.

Z: Look carefully, and you'll see a couple of New Zealand natives peering out at you: the ubiquitous sheep.

E: Three different home-produced fabrics inspired by the iridescent colours and wavy lines of the paua shell.

A selection of New Zealand fabrics at The Quilters' Barn, Blenheim

A: Fruit, glorious fruit: not only the inevitable kiwifruit, but some little apples alongside too.

L: The silver fern, official symbol of the All Blacks, looks dramatic against a black background.

A: More ferns, showing just how versatile these plants are as design motifs.

N: In the shadows, could that possibly be an elusive kiwi or three?

D: Water, water everywhere – and where there's water, there's seafood!

Find out more …

Many homegrown New Zealand fabrics are produced by Nutex (www.nutex.co.nz); browse these and lots of other Kiwi fabrics at the UK shop Kiwiana (www.kiwiana.uk), and at www.kiwiquilts.co.nz.

THE TECHNIQUE

A good satin stitch is the key to a good crisp outline for these letters. There are various little tricks that will help you to produce a good satin stitch: here are my top tips. First of all, attach the shape you're stitching securely to the background; this way, it can't move out of position while you're stitching it, and you're not going to get lots of wisps of thread (what I call 'moustaches') sticking up through the satin stitch. Either use bonding web on the back of the cut shapes (as I did for the letters), or stitch the edges of the patch down with a small machine zigzag. Then, when you're ready to do the satin stitch, use a piece of tearaway foundation fabric (or a piece of cartridge paper) behind the stitching; this helps to stop it undulating. If you have a Bernina machine, put the bobbin thread through the little hole at the end of the arm on the bobbin-case before you start sewing; this gives your satin stitch an extra-smooth finish.

SEASCAPE

In New Zealand the sea is never far away, presenting an unending display of seascapes as the light and the weather conditions change.

If you've seen the second Narnia film, *Prince Caspian*, you probably remember the transformation near the beginning when the dirty, dark railway station metamorphoses into a cave near crystalline turquoise water. And that truly is the colour of the New Zealand sea – it's very clear and clean, and the colours are an ever-changing theatre of teal and navy (apparently that's why Air New Zealand chose those colours for their uniforms).

There are so many beaches that even in summer it's not hard to find one that you can have virtually to yourself; on our first day ever in the country we strolled barefoot along the sands of Auckland's north shore, picking up smooth stones and shards of paua shell (see p20) as we looked across to the city skyline (see p22) – not something that you'd be in a rush to do along the banks of the Thames. Three years later we spent New Year's Eve on the beaches of the Abel Tasman national park, near Nelson, where the sand varies from almost white on some parts of the shoreline to caramel-coloured on others. On the Coromandel Peninsula we strolled along seaside roads fringed with pohutukawa trees (see p18), and took a bus ride round the spectacular

Beaches at Waihi (above) and the Abel Tasman National Park

coastline near Coromandel itself. In Picton, the south island port for the inter-island ferry, the energetic can climb to The Snout, the tip of the peninsula that sticks out into the Queen Charlotte Sound. (In Maori The Snout is known as *Te Ihumoeoneihu*, which means 'the nose of the sandworm.') From this peninsula you get breathtaking views

of bush-covered hills dipping into the sapphire-coloured sea, and it's easy to imagine yourself back several hundred years, to the days when the first explorers landed on the islands.

My seascape is an amalgam of lots of these views; the background is a simple bit of stitch-and-flip piecing, to which I've added depth by layering it with randomly-cut strips sheer fabrics. Intensive quilting creates the texture and pattern of the waves, and added beads catch the light and create the effect of sun glinting on the water's surface.

Find out more ...

www.teara.govt.nz is the online encyclopedia of New Zealand, which is packed with intriguing information; go there and click on the Earth, Sea and Sky section to access all kinds of details of the country's natural history.

MAKE YOUR OWN

If you'd like to create your own version of *Seascape*, you'll find the instructions on page 77.

If you'd like to create your own version of *Seascape*, you'll find the instructions on page 77.

INSIDE INFORMATION

Materials

Cotton, silk and synthetic fabrics, including sheers and velvets; beads, cords, shell fragments

Quilting

On the sea areas I've added lots of wiggly wave lines in embroidery threads and couched cords; on the sand pieces I've quilted a flowing design to give the impression of ripples made by the receding tide.

Backing and binding

The backing for the design is a piece of plain turquoise fabric, and the layers are bound with a strip of emerald-green silk, which picks up both the colour and the sheen of the seascape.

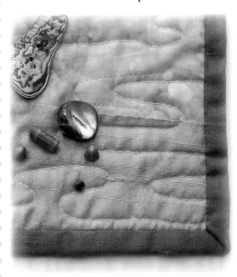

Materials

Cotton batik and marbled fabrics

Quilting

To keep the dynamic of the spiral, I quilted wavy lines of machine quilting outward from the centre, breaking the lines at each circle so that the stone shapes stood out in relief. For extra emphasis I quilted round each circle individually, too.

Backing and binding

I used the same fabric for the backing and the binding – a brown fabric covered in random sandy-coloured dots, which themselves look like small pebbles.

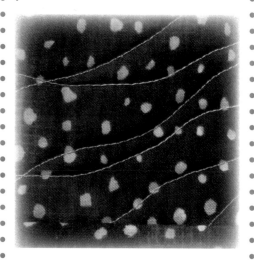

STONE SPIRAL

A dramatic spiral of rocks is half-decoration, half-sculpture.

Spiral sculptures at Rapaura Water Gardens (above) and Russell (right)

Not many artefacts survive from the early history of New Zealand's Maori people, as their traditional buildings are made of wood and don't last through the centuries, but it's safe to assume that the settlements early white explorers discovered had been pretty much unchanged for generations. At Kerikeri (see p54) there is a *pa* with artists' impressions of what the Maori settlement on it would have looked like in the early 19th century – and it's disconcertingly like the artists' impressions of the neolithic flint mines in our Sussex homeland – several millennia earlier!

One thing that always seems to have been important to the Maori people is the symbol of the spiral, which appears in different forms in much of their art – the prows of their war canoes are carved in intricate spirals, and many of their *moko* designs (see p40) echo the same form. Sometimes these spirals are stylised into what have become known as *koru* curls.

The spiral is such a strong visual device, I wanted to devote a whole quilt to it, and decided to build my spiral in stones of different colours and sizes. I made the stones circular to echo a phenomenon we didn't actually get to see, but have seen photographs of: the boulders on the beach at Moeraki, north of Dunedin. These massive rocks are almost perfect hemispheres, which make the beach look as though the gods have abandoned a giant game of marbles on the shore: according to Maori legend the boulders are the food baskets from a canoe wrecked on the coast in ancient times.

So that I could obtain a realistic look, I didn't want to use fabrics that featured regular prints. A pack of assorted batiks in neutral tones provided a wide range of mottled and randomly-coloured fabrics which made perfect stones. To make the stone shapes look as though they were 3D, I also padded the circles with extra discs of wadding and gave each one a shadow in dark brown. All the shadows were cut from the same dark brown fabric, and appliquéd to the background first, before I added the stone shapes on top. The brown ferny background batik was a good foil for the different fabrics I'd used for the rest of the design. I attached my shapes using invisible machine appliqué, but if you make your own version (see p78) you'll find it easier to use bonding web – easier, quicker, and less fiddly!

Find out more ...

www.toiiho.com is the website of a gallery specialising in contemporary Maori art

To find out more about stone in Maori life, go to www. teara.govt.nz and tap in 'Maori use of stone'.

MAKE YOUR OWN

If you'd like to create your own version of *Stone Spiral*, you'll find the instructions on page 78.

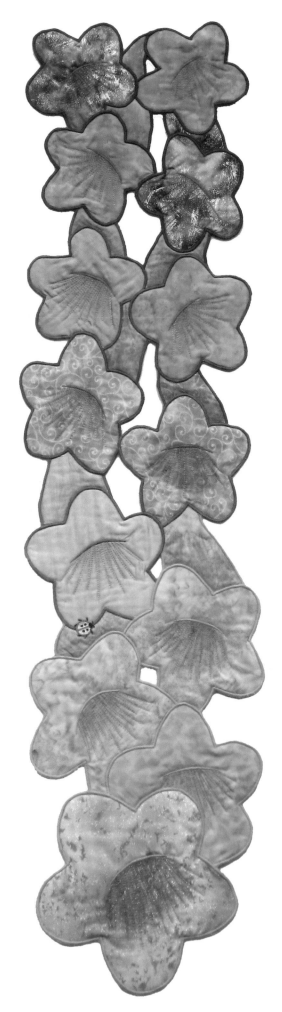

JACARANDA

A sprig of purple-blue blossoms in machine cutwork looks rather like an oriental flower arrangement.

I've occasionally seen jacaranda trees in other countries (including one very sad specimen in England), but never as abundantly as they appeared in NZ. I couldn't stop photographing these beautiful trees – they look lovely against the blue sky, but the fallen blossoms also create a pretty-coloured confetti on the ground.

Because these trees tend to have most of their flowers before their leaves, they have a rather oriental feel, which tied in with another strand of New Zealand life. In recent years the country has seen a large influx of Asian people – many of them have come as students, then perhaps stayed to raise a family, or brought over their own families from

Materials

Cotton plain, print and marbled fabrics, fabric paint

Quilting

The edges of the flowers are sealed with satin stitch, which quilts them at the same time; for the flower centres I added some depth with fabric crayon, then quilted each one with random-length lines of straight machine stitching.

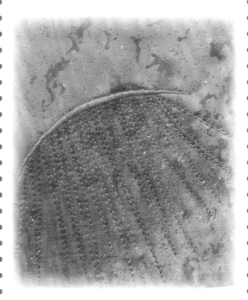

the Asian subcontinent. Not surprisingly, this eastern influence has infiltrated many aspects of New Zealand life – cuisine, art, architecture etc – so I thought I would give my jacaranda branch a touch of the orient.

The flowers are made from a variety of different purple fabrics, shading from dark at the top of the branch to paler for the larger, more mature flowers at the tip of the branch; around each blossom I've worked machine satin stitch in a shade that complements the fabric. I created the flower centres with a mixture of fabric painting and machine quilting, to give depth to the long trumpet-shaped flowers. And the final touch: I found a mauve-tinted ladybird motif at just the right size.

Find out more ...

If you'd like to know more about the different people-groups that make up the modern Kiwi population, go to www.teara.govt.nz and follow the links to New Zealand Peoples (byline: 'discover the people who made New Zealand home').

Backing and edging

The backing is a single piece of one of the fabrics I used for the blossoms; the edges of the quilt are shaped round the individual flowers by the lines of machine satin stitch.

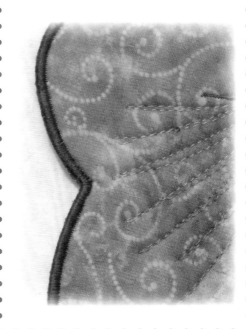

THE TECHNIQUE

To create a good crisp cutwork outline, first of all stitch round the relevant edge with a small machine zigzag. Use small, sharp-pointed scissors to trim the layers back to the line of zigzag (it doesn't matter if you snip one or two of the stitches – you're going to go over them with more stitching). Position a layer of Stitch 'n' Tear or other tearaway foundation paper behind the work, then follow the tips on page 7 for producing a good satin stitch around the cut edge. Carefully tear away the foundation paper to leave the satin stitch edge.

MAORI CURVES

The classic colours and curved lines of traditional Maori designs are captured in this dramatic quilt.

If you visit a *whare runanga,* the meeting house that is at the centre of the traditional *marae* (meeting place), you'll find it decorated in various ways. Inside you'll see panels created from New Zealand flax, woven into all kinds of intricate patterns (see page 50). Long poles carved with figures represent the tribal ancestors and chieftains. Outside, under the gable roof of the meeting house, there will be wooden panels painted in distinctive curvilinear designs coloured red, white and black. Presumably the pigments to create these paints were the easiest to get hold of when the Maori first arrived on the islands. At first sight these designs look a bit like paisley patterns; although there are endless variations, the basic shapes are curved and pointed white lines which meander across red and black backgrounds.

The distinctive shapes of these designs are traditionally inspired by the head of the hammerhead shark. According to legend, when the Maori were first travelling to their new land, hammerhead sharks circled their rafts and kept them safe from the more voracious predator sharks – who were presumably looking on the visitors as a kind of

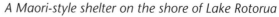

A Maori-style shelter on the shore of Lake Rotorua

A traditional Maori design decorates a ceiling in Napier

floating buffet. In gratitude for this protection, the Maori have immortalised the hammerhead in their tattoos (see p40) and also in these red/black/white patterns. In this quilt I've taken a strip down a traditional Maori pattern and interpreted it in my signature technique, stained glass patchwork; I've used slightly patterned fabrics for my red, black and white areas, which create more visual interest than plain fabrics would.

Find out more ...

Maori Art and Culture edited by Davidson and Starzecka, ISBN 9781869533021; also, go to www.teara.govt.nz and click on the section called Maori New Zealanders.

The marae *at Waitangi, with the only pan-tribal* whare runanga

MAKE YOUR OWN

If you'd like to create your own version of *Maori Curves*, you'll find the instructions on page 79.

You'll find the instructions on page 79.

INSIDE INFORMATION

Materials
Red, white and black cotton print fabrics

Quilting
I embellished the white patches with lines of machine quilting down the centre, and added a line of red machine stitching along the outside borders. The lines of the design were emphasised by outlining each patch in big-stitch quilting worked in a contrasting colour of coton à broder.

Binding
To bind the edges I used a red print fabric that's subtly different from the red print used in the quilt; it includes tiny black motifs and flecks of gold.

Backing
A mottled red-and-black fabric shows off the lines of hand-quilting and the decorative machine-quilting stitches.

INSIDE INFORMATION

Materials
Synthetic and wool felts, buttons

Quilting
The decorative machine stitches which embellish the patches are also the quilting stitches, as they go through all the layers.

Backing and edging
The backing is another layer of pale blue felt. To edge the quilt I cut strips of different-coloured felts into decorative borders, using a different design for each strip; these give the design a bit of a fairground feel. I appliquéd and embellished the borders with machine stitching and more tiny buttons.

A quaint bird, created in bright embroidered felts, peers out from among the bulrushes.

The kiwi is, of course, the official bird of New Zealand, but it's rarely seen for several reasons. First of all, kiwi are quite rare; there are only a few places in the country where you can see them in their natural habitat. Secondly they're quite shy. Thirdly, they're nocturnal. So your chances of bumping into one while you're out doing your daily constitutional are quite slim. As a result, the pukeko seems to have become the unofficial official bird, decorating all manner of tourist souvenirs.

If you've never seen a pukeko, picture a large, plump, blue coot or moorhen. Yes, that wasn't a typing error: I did say blue. This absurd bird (also known less poetically as the New Zealand Swamp Hen) is a member of the rail family; it

This delightful fabric is called Pukeko Swamp (Nutex7099)

has glossy navy blue plumage, and brown or red legs, plus a red beak. Chris says that pukekos always look as though they think someone's following them, walking their high-stepping walk while peering round with their beady eyes. Like their cousins in the UK they love water, and can be seen pootling round the edges of ponds, lakes and rivers. When we took a boat ride down the river in Blenheim, drifting through the local vineyards as we did our best to sample as much local food and wine as possible, these

delightful companions were dabbling all round the edges of the water: as the captain said in inimitable Kiwi: 'Pukekos. As cute as, eh?'

As they're such cartoon birds, I decided to make them into a cartoony quilt: I used brightly-coloured felts, layering the shapes on top of each other to create a kind of mola feel. By using felt, of course, you don't need to neaten the edges in any way. I chose synthetic felts for the most part, as they're thinner than the traditional

woollen felts and it's possible to cut the patches with sharper edges. I used fancy machine stitches in contrasting colours to attach the patches and quilt the work in one go; because the felt is quite thin I could go through several layers at a time when necessary. As the felts themselves create a padded surface, I didn't add a separate wadding layer. I set my pukeko in two of the beautiful plants we saw around various lakes and streams – bulrushes and water-lilies – and gave him a butterfly and dragonfly for company. To create the stems of the bulrushes I used machine stitching over a fine cord; I felt that a simple line of satin stitch would have disappeared into the felt. Tiny plastic buttons in bright colours add the finishing touches to various parts of the design.

Find out more …

Auckland Zoological Gardens houses many species of native New Zealand birds and animals (as well as animals from other countries), and is one place where you can see the elusive kiwi: www.aucklandzoo.co.nz. In Auckland Regional Botanic Gardens you can admire 10,000 species of native and introduced plants.

MAKE YOUR OWN

If you'd like to create your own version of *Pukeko*,
you'll find the instructions on page 80.

POHUTUKAWA

Scarlet flowers and deep green leaves decorate the 'New Zealand Christmas Tree.'

During the summer months (which of course in New Zealand include Christmas), the coasts of the north island in particular are decorated by the vivid pohutukawa tree (*Metrosideros excelsa*). It took me two weeks to learn how to say its name, and even longer to learn how to spell it. A relative of the myrtle, the pohutukawa's vivid red blooms are formed from hundreds of scarlet fronds, each one tipped with a tiny yellow globe; the foliage is glossy green, so this combination of seasonal colours has led to its popular name: the New Zealand Christmas tree. (We did see a few trees with yellow blossoms, too, but they're not nearly so common.)

At Cape Reinga, the northernmost tip of the country where the Pacific Ocean meets the Tasman Sea, there's a very ancient pohutukawa tree thought by some people to be 800 years old; in Maori belief that's the spot at which the spirits of the dead depart, travelling down the roots of the tree to begin their journey back to the land of Hawaiki (traditionally the homeland of Tupe – see page 74).

It took me a while to decide how to interpret the pohutukawa in stitchery. Lots of lines of machine quilting didn't seem quite 3D enough, and the flowers are too delicate and ethereal to be done as a piece of solid appliqué. After a bit of experimentation I found the solution: the blooms are built up from layers of different

Materials

Cotton and synthetic fabrics, beads

Quilting

The blossoms themselves are stitched with lines of wavy machining in red; this both holds the sheer fabrics in place and quilts the blossoms. Inside and outside the edges of the appliquéd green stems, calyxes and leaves, and inside the border, I've worked lines of hand quilting in green.

Backing

Another New Zealand fabric, this time celebrating the pohutukawa tree in all its glory.

Binding

A Christmassy print echoes the festive feel of the blossoms and leaves; I made the border a little wider on this quilt so that it plays more of a part in the overall design.

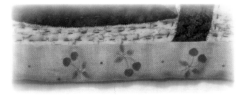

red sheers, cut into ragged circles then folded into quarters. I tucked these shapes behind the green calyx shapes of the flowers; the red sheers spill out from the calyxes just like the actual blossoms. I anchored the red sheers with some wavy lines of red stitching, then added yellow beads to create the tips of the fronds. To maintain the Christmassy feel I used a cream and gold print for the background, and bound the edges in a seasonal print.

I used invisible machine appliqué for the leaves and calyxes, pressing the fabric over freezer paper templates; if you fancy making your own version of the quilt (see below) you can do it this way, but to keep it simpler I've suggested that you use bonding web appliqué instead.

Find out more ...

www.opotiki.com/data/pohutuka.htm will tell you all kinds of different things about the humble pohutukawa.

If you go to www.teara.govt.nz and tap in Hawaiki, you'll find more about the traditional homeland of the Maori.

MAKE YOUR OWN

If you'd like to create your own version of *Pohutukawa*, you'll find the instructions on page 81.

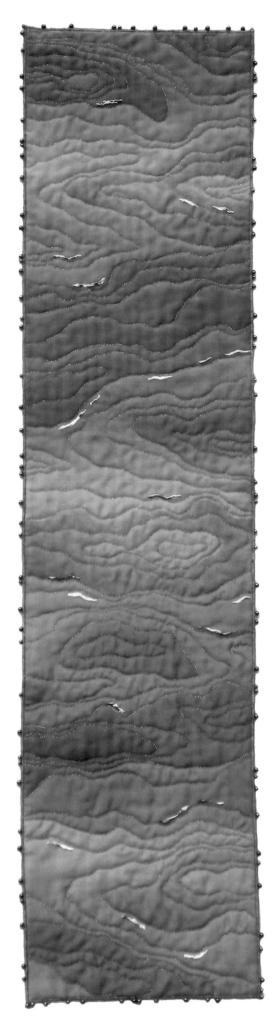

ÞAUA

A *sliver of iridescent shell gleams in the sunlight.*

Not surprisingly, as the water around New Zealand teems with life, the beaches are rich in shells of different kinds. Just as in the UK, beaches in different areas offer up different collections of shells, creating their own decorative collages on the shorelines. One mollusc in particular has always been prized by the Maori because it holds a double treasure: paua shell, or abalone, is found all round the shores of NZ. If you stroll along the beaches you're likely to find sea-sculpted shards of this iridescent nacre – like a rainbow-coloured mother-of-pearl.

The Maori use paua as a food source, but also prize it particularly as a material for decorative arts; slices of paua form the eyes of the slightly creepy little *tiki*, dumpy figures (often with their tongues sticking out) which adorn many Maori carvings. Maori woodcarving can be exquisite; complex patterns adorn the heads of war canoes and the rafters of meeting houses. It can also be quite grotesque, like the gargoyles on our cathedrals – grimacing heads (often with paua-shell eyes) would guard the palisades of the *pa*, the name for the traditional Maori fortified village built on a mound. The red colour often used to coat the wood carvings was historically made from red pigment mixed with whale oil, although in later years red paint has obscured most of the ancient colouring.

It's become so popular as a decorative material that rules have been brought in to restrict the number of entire paua that can be gathered (generally 10 a day). Jewellery made from paua shell is available all over New Zealand, and it's also often set into woodcarvings and other decorative arts. I've included a piece of paua on my *Seascape* quilt (see page 8), and you can also see slices of the shell gleaming in the light in the little Maori-style building shown on page 14.

My slice of paua shell is built up from layers of sheer fabrics; I picked several different shaded polyesters, as the synthetic weave catches the light well. I began with one large background rectangle and covered it with shapes I'd cut randomly from other colourways; as the colours of the fabrics intermingled they created extra colours across the design. I finished off with another complete rectangle to seal in all the cut edges, then machine-quilted round the edges of the different shaded areas. Iridescent beads and tiny touches of foiling added to the quilt's light-catching qualities.

Find out more ...

www.nzmaori.co.nz is the website of the New Zealand Maori Arts and Crafts Institute, in the Whakarewarewa area of Rotorua, where woodcarvers and flax weavers (see page 50) can be seen at work.

www.pauamania.com will tell you all kinds of things about paua shell and some of the items that can be made with it

www.oceanshellnz.com has some lovely examples of paua-shell jewellery

THE TECHNIQUE

Foiling is a great way of adding highlights to a design. There are various systems on the market, but they all work in a similar way. A white glue is applied to the area(s) you want to cover with foil; when it's dry the glue is clear, but still tacky. The special plastic foil is laid on top of the glue and rubbed/pressed gently; the foil adheres to the glued area, leaving a metallic shape when the foil sheet is lifted away.

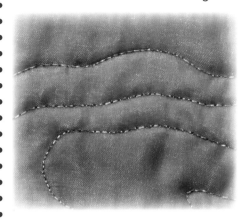

Materials

Bright cotton print and marbled fabrics, beads and buttons

Quilting

To suggest the idea of bungy-jumping, I quilted the design from top to bottom in wavy lines; the multicoloured thread picks up all the different colours of the patches.

Backing and binding

The quilt is backed with plain white cotton. For the binding I cut the edges of the quilt into waves to echo the quilting lines, and rounded the corners, then bound it with a gorgeous bright multicoloured bias binding – it had to be on the bias, of course, to ease round the curves.

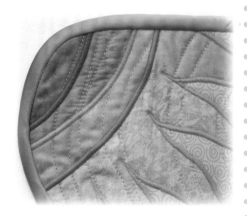

SKY TOWER

Yes, it's the Sky Tower – but not as you know it!

Auckland's distinctive skyline, seen across the water from Devonport

The skyline of Auckland is very distinctive: you can always easily identify it in photographs. First of all you've got the large rectangular tower with a halo on top, which is the Vero building; then you'll also see the inevitable tall tower (no doubt the result of typical macho tower-envy: 'mine's bigger than yours …'). Auckland's Sky Tower was opened in 1997, and at 328m (1,076ft) high is the tallest building in the southern hemisphere. Apparently from the sky deck and the rotating restaurant at the top of the tower you can see 50 miles on a clear day – I'm quite happy to take other people's word for that, as even looking at the tower from the ground gives me vertigo.

Believe it or not, people actually bungy-jump from the Sky Tower – not head first, thank goodness, as the tower's in the middle of the city streets, but in a standing star shape supported by several cables. Bungy-jumping (sometimes spelt bungee-jumping), that most extraordinary of modern pastimes, began in New Zealand and is now copied all over the world. Its historic origins, though, are in the Pacific Islands, where it's still practised as a coming-of-age ritual and to help ensure a good yam harvest.

Personally, I don't like the Sky Tower building very much: I think it looks like a hypodermic syringe. But as it's so iconic, and especially as all my quilts were long and thin, I knew I had to include a Sky Tower design. But I decided that I didn't want it to be a straight depiction of the tower as it actually is; I wanted something less steely, more quirky – a kind of funky, hippy Sky Tower. You know those

The Sky Tower seen from the wharf

seminal photographs of the 1960s, during the Peace Movement, of flowers being put in the barrels of soldiers' guns? That was the kind of zany image I wanted, with bright pop-culture prints and colours, complemented by the multicoloured binding. I drew a cartoony version of the building, then used machine satin stitch in contrasting colours to appliqué the patches to the background; to soften the design still more, I used a sunshiny yellow background and added a funky sun and a cheerful Bird of Paradise (*strelizia*) flower. For a final hippy overlay the design was embellished with lots of 60s-look coloured plastic beads and buttons.

Find out more …
www.skycityauckland.co.nz is the Sky Tower's official website

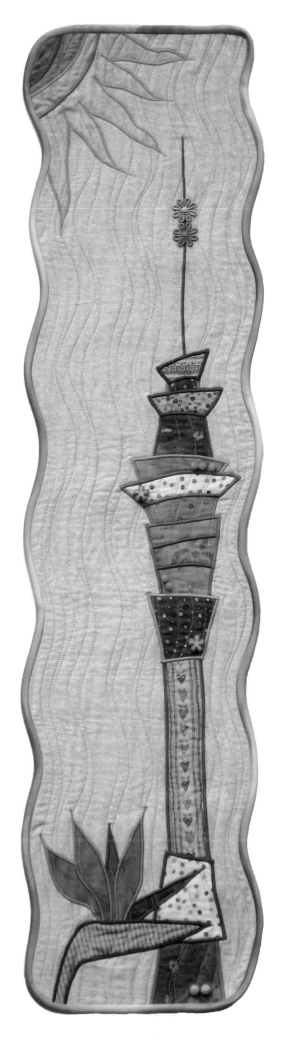

MAKE YOUR OWN
If you'd like to create your own version of *Sky Tower*, you'll find the instructions on page 82.

NEW ZEALAND TARTAN

The Celtic heritage of many Kiwis is celebrated in a colourful plaid.

A quarter of present-day New Zealanders can trace their ancestry directly back to Scottish Presbyterian stock, and many others to Irish roots. People left Scotland and Ireland in their droves during the 18th and 19th centuries: the Highland Clearances; the repeated failure of the potato harvest (which, although often known as the Irish Potato Famine, affected impoverished Scots almost as much); and, not least, the emigration of the breakaway Free Church of Scotland to find more religious freedom.

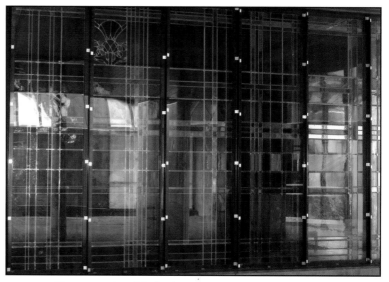

Tartan and a thistle decorating a Dunedin building

These Celtic people scattered to England, to America, and also in quite large numbers to New Zealand (often by way of Australia). And when you see the hills of the south island, you can see why they felt so at home; apart from the odd sprouting of New Zealand flax, you could be in Ireland's Achill Sound or Scotland's Glencoe. I felt that it would be fitting to celebrate this heritage by creating my own New Zealand tartan, to echo the plaids worn by these historic families – again, although tartan is mostly associated with Scotland, Irish clans also have their own tartans (and often wear them in the form of kilts).

This is actually the only quilt in the whole series that I remade. The original version was created in purple, emerald, turquoise and blue, quilted with spirals and embroidered lines; although it was very attractive in itself, somehow it didn't quite capture the feeling I was trying to convey. It seemed too bright. I had a whole series of fabric tubes left over from a previous project (what is patchwork after all, if not recycling?!), and I felt that they would make a more convincing tartan with greater depth and

Scottish-style landscape (and sea mist!) near Dunedin

richness – and so it proved. The rich background colours gave the design more body, and the gold streaks pick up that idea of looking for a newer, more prosperous life – see also the quilt *Gold* on page 58. The fact that I'd used a series of fabrics from the same range seemed to give the quilt more visual unity, while still providing strands of many different colours.

Find out more ...

The book *Going Abroad* by John MacGibbon is a history of Scots migration to New Zealand; its blurb says that it 'traces the hopes, fears and fortunes of early Scottish migrants to New Zealand's Deep South.' It's published by Ngaio Press (www.ngaiopress.com), ISBN 0958224431.

THE TECHNIQUE

I used 3½in (9cm)-wide strips of fabric, which I stitched into tubes and turned out; I pressed them to flatten them and set the edges, then decorated some with gold braids. As I wove them I kept the strips in position with pins; the quilting lines then also did the secondary job of stabilising the weave so that the final piece doesn't distort.

INSIDE INFORMATION

Materials

Cotton fabrics, metallic braids

Quilting

I worked straight(ish) lines of machine stitching in gold across the quilt both vertically and horizontally; these lines of stitching both quilted the design and stablised the warp and weft strips.

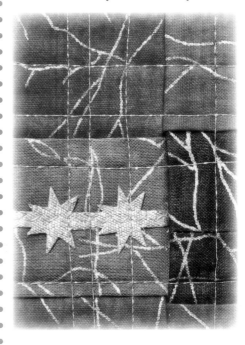

Backing and edging

No separate backing was necessary for the woven design. I left the ends of the strips raw, but trimmed them with pinking shears to create the impression of a swatch of plaid fabric.

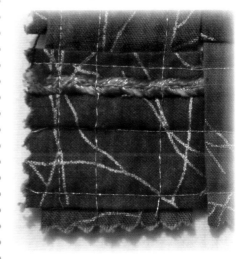

A Norfolk Pine on the seafront in Napier

FLORA

Papercut repeats of four distinctive New Zealand plants create blocks that echo the country's Pacific Island influences.

As well as the spectacular flowers of New Zealand (see pages 5, 52-53 and 56-57), there are many other distinctive plants and trees that are endlessly fascinating, and I wanted to celebrate some of those in a quilt all to themselves. Many of the Pacific Islands have their own versions of papercut quilt designs – the *Tivaevae* of the Cook Islands, the *Kapa Lau* of Hawaii etc – all based on stylised versions of the local plant life. Even if you've never created a quilt this way you'll have used the technique: remember those papercut snowflakes we all did at primary school? When you fold a piece of paper into four, or six, and cut holes in it, then unfold it to produce a lovely lacy design? In *Flora* I've created my own papercut designs from some of the plants we enjoyed seeing, echoing the Pacific Island heritage of the Maori.

Once I'd had the basic idea, I had to pick the plants I wanted to feature. The fern was an obvious one – even though I'd included ferns on several other quilts (see pages 62 and 64), I felt I hadn't exhausted their design potential. I wanted to include a Norfolk Pine, too; these trees pop up all over the country, and we particularly enjoyed seeing them in Napier, where their highly stylised shapes seemed to complement the Art Deco architecture perfectly. New

Zealand flax seemed an obvious inclusion, both because of its distinctive shape (like a yucca with spindly fingers of red flowers coming out of the top), and because of its importance to the Maori for their weaving. And we fell in love with the New Zealand cabbage trees, too, with their mops of spiky leaves that look like Dennis the Menace's haircut.

Flax plant, Botanic Gardens, Napier

So, I had the four plants for my four blocks, but how was I going to interpret them? Fiddly needleturning of the edges is most definitely not my technique, and I also felt that many of the lines would be too fine for successful machine appliqué. I pondered this for several weeks, then the revelation came: sunprinting. This process involves laying stencil shapes over fabric prepared with light-sensitive chemicals, then – as the name suggests – laying the fabric in the sun; where the stencils are, the fabric remains pale, and where the sun reaches the fabric it becomes a deep blue (rather like the effect of sunbathing in a swimsuit when the sun doesn't tan the areas under your swimsuit straps).

The stencils can be cut shapes, leaves, flowers etc; I obviously wanted to use my papercut shapes. Then came the second inspiration; if I cut the shapes from freezer paper, that would enable me to iron the cut shapes firmly against the fabric, which would ensure that the sun couldn't creep under the edges of the stencil and would keep the edges of the shapes really crisp. I pressed the cut shapes on two of the squares of prepared fabric; I knew that these would produce white shapes on blue backgrounds. For the other two blocks I discarded the plant shape itself, and used its 'negative' – the paper from outside the shape – to create a blue shape on a pale background. The alternation of the positive and negative blocks gives the finished quilt a strong graphic quality. I also positioned a layer of lace across all the squares while they were 'curing' in the sun, which created an extra depth to the texture.

Find out more ...

If you'd like to try your own sunprinting projects, Rainbow Silks sell ready-prepared fabric, and also the chemicals necessary to prepare your own: www.rainbowsilks.com

---

MAKE YOUR OWN

If you'd like to create your own version of *Flora*, you'll find the instructions on pages 84-85.

INSIDE INFORMATION

Materials

White cotton fabric prepared with cyanotype chemicals

Quilting

Pacific Island papercut quilts often use echo quilting – stitching around the outline of the design and then adding other lines to echo the original one. I've done my own version by machine, using white thread on the pale backgrounds and blue on the dark backgrounds.

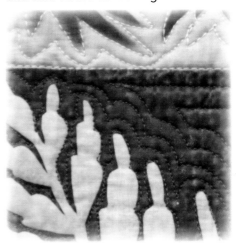

Binding

It took me a while to find just the right fabric for the binding. After sunprinting the pale areas of the fabric aren't pure white, but a soft misty blue; as a result, most blue-and-white print fabrics look too stark. Eventually I tried this silvery print fabric; the blues were just right, and the softness of the print complemented the gentle blues of the blocks.

Backing

White cotton with a creamy floral print; the white quilting lines blend into it, and the blue lines create a strong contrast.

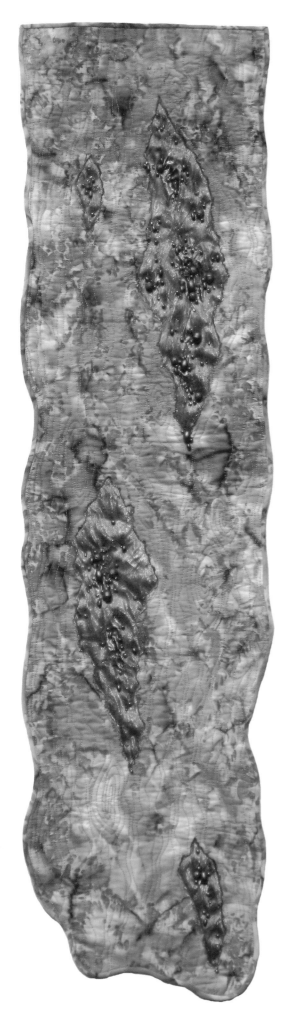

KAURI

An evocation of that ancient guardian of the forests – the kauri.

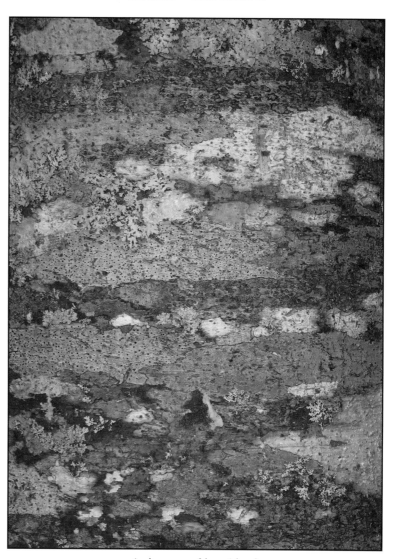

A close-up of kauri bark

When the first white settlers came to New Zealand, one of the things they prized about the country was its kauri trees. These giants are some of the largest trees in the world; the largest kauri are believed to be 1,500-2,000 years old, and many are over 1,000 years old. Because the trees are slow-growing, and therefore have very hard wood, the timber was excellent for shipbuilding (including mastmaking), housebuilding and carving. Trade abounded, with ship after ship leaving laden with kauri logs – but the kauri also provided another, less obvious treasure too.

Where trees had fallen and exuded their resin, they produced harvests of amber-coloured kauri gum, which could be dug up in lumps and sold for use as lacquer (rather like shellac) and for ornaments (like amber); carved pieces of kauri gum still make popular souvenirs. The way to find these nuggets was to prod the areas surrounding dead kauri trees with long rods until they hit pockets of gum which could then be dug out. By 1885, there were around 2,000 gumdiggers in the country. One rainy day we sat in the tiny local museum in Thames, on the Coromandel Peninsula, and leafed through loose-leaf files filled with photographs of woodsmen sitting wide-legged astride vast kauri logs, and whole families of gumdiggers armed with spades.

The kauri tree is now protected throughout the country. In the south island they're pretty rare; near the rather romantically- (and slightly inaccurately-) named Centre of New Zealand, outside Nelson (pictured at the bottom of page 4), you can find a solitary and rather small kauri, but in the north island it's possible to visit whole forests of these old men of the bush; the Waipoua Forest in Northland has superb specimens. The kauri bark is variegated and unusual, and its wood is beautifully grained; I decided to combine these attributes with the idea of the hidden treasure of the gum associated with the trees. The random-dyed brown background fabric was a great jumping-off point for the suggestion of bark, and I quilted a woodgrain design into it, then added a suggestion of amber gum almost dripping out of the tree like jewelled nectar. (I made these pieces from layers of sheer fabric, cutting the shapes with the tip of a soldering iron.) The beading on the amber sections incorporates some chippings of real kauri gum.

Find out more ...

www.kauri-museum.com

THE TECHNIQUE

Soldering irons have appeared in the quilt world in increasing numbers over recent years, and they're great for this kind of work when you want an uneven shape. Not only can you create any shape you want, including very detailed ones, but the soldering iron seals the edges of the fabrics too, preventing them from fraying. I layered several sheer fabrics in amber colours then traced a  wiggly outline with the soldering iron; the resulting random shapes were then all ready to be appliquéd to the quilt and embellished. If you're trying this, remember to follow all the safety precautions specified by the soldering iron's manufacturer – and remember too that this method only works on synthetic fabrics; it won't cut through cotton.

INSIDE INFORMATION

Materials

Batik cotton fabric, synthetic sheer fabrics, beads, chips of kauri gum

Quilting

The background features a closely-stitched woodgrain design; I didn't mark this design but simply stitched it intuitively, moving the fabric under the free machining foot to create a pattern of grain and spiral knots in the 'wood.'

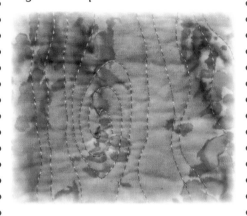

Backing and binding

The quilt is backed with a simple layer of brown fabric. I trimmed the edges of the quilt into random shapes to suggest a piece of bark pulled off a tree, or a rough piece of wood found in the forest. The raw edges were then bound with a very narrow bias binding, using a double-folded strip of fabric. To create this very fine binding, I stitched the raw edges of the folded strip to the wavy edges of the quilt, using a small machine stitch for security, then trimmed back to about 2mm away from the stitching; the folded edge of the binding could then be turned to the back, leaving only a very small amount of fabric on the front.

• Materials

Assorted cotton and polyester/cotton fabrics

Quilting

Because the layers of fabric were quite thick by this stage, I quilted the shapes simply by machine, using a wavy automatic stitch to edge each grape several times and to create lines on the vineleaf.

Backing and binding

A simple print fabric in a pale purple-blue colour worked well for the backing. I tried green fabrics around the quilted design but they detracted from the colour in the grapes and blended too much into the leaf – purple fabrics presented similar problems the other way around. A mottled fabric which mixed tones of purple and green proved the perfect choice, and the little gold fleck made it subtly different from the rest of the quilt without clashing.

GRAPES

Succulent grapes, sun-warmed and perfectly ripe, hang from the vine just ready for harvesting.

The first vine in New Zealand was planted by James Busby (1800-71), when he was the official British Resident of the country, in the garden of his delightful wooden residence in Waitangi. This was the backdrop to the signing of the Treaty of Waitangi on February 6th 1840, when Maori chieftains officially signed over sovereignty of the country to the British Crown. It's possible still to visit this little colonial house at the Treaty Grounds in the

Gail in the Treaty House gardens at Waitangi

beautiful Bay of Islands; in the grounds you'll find *Ngatoki Matawhaorua* (the largest wooden war canoe in the world), a Maori meeting house or *whare runanga*, and a spectacular view across the bay. The original vine disappeared long ago, but we know that it was used to create the first documented New Zealand wine; Busby was a trained vintner. Thus began an industry that has gone from strength to strength in recent years, with NZ wines winning many awards.

The soil and other conditions lend themselves to both red and white wines, with different areas specialising in each. The best-known wine-growing regions are Hawke's Bay on the North Island, and Marlborough in the south island; it's possible to take tasting tours that visit 36 different vineyards (although Chris maintains that you actually only visit ten; after that you're too drunk to notice that you're going round the same ones again …). The Wither Hills near Blenheim in the south island have given their name to a delicious wine which (along with many other NZ wines) you can find in UK shops; the label features the very distinctive hills, which are covered in a dry brownish grass. Or, if you want to avoid the hangover, you can simply buy and eat the grapes!

I wanted to give this quilt an impressionistic feel, so I picked out lots of mottled and batiked fabrics in shades of purple,

Vineyards in front of the Wither Hills near Blenheim

mauve and green, and backed them with bonding web. I then cut them into roughly oval patches with pinking shears, so that the edges of the patches would blend into each other. On a thin white backing fabric I drew the design of the grapes and vine leaf, then built up the grapes so that they shaded from dark to light through the bunch, and each grape looked plump and rounded; once I'd built up two or three grapes I ironed the patches to fuse them in place. Each grape is finished off with a shaped highlight patch to give the impression of the sunlight gleaming on its skin. Once the entire design had been created, I layered it and added some simple machine quilting.

Find out more ...

For more information on the Waitangi Treaty Ground, visit www.waitangi.net.nz

For more information about the country's wines, visit www.nzwine,com

---

THE TECHNIQUE

I used pinking shears to cut the rough ovals from the different fabrics; crimping the edges in this way means that the shapes are softened when you overlap them, which helps the colours blend into an attractive Impressionist-style arrangement.

NAPIER BEAUTY

The geometric shapes of a traditional block have been adapted here into a celebration of Art Deco.

I used to hate Art Deco – Odeon architecture, as it's often called in the UK because so many cinemas were built at the height of its popularity. But we visited one place in New Zealand which changed my mind instantly – and if you've been there, you'll know the place I mean. It's called Napier, and it's known as the Art Deco jewel of the north island.

So, what's so special about it? If it hadn't been for one fateful day 80 years ago, Napier would probably be a relatively unremarkable middle-sized town, carrying on its everyday business, but at 10.47am on February 3rd 1931 an earthquake measuring 7.8 on the Richter scale shook the town to its core, literally and metaphorically. The epicentre was only 15-20km north of Napier: 162 townspeople died, and the centre of the town was badly damaged, both by the quake and by the fires that gutted many buildings in the aftermath. Napier had been on a peninsula of land, almost an island, and had been working hard to reclaim some of the nearby low-lying swamp land

Art Deco details on buildings in Hastings (above) and Napier

from the water so that it could expand: ironically, the movement of the tectonic plates created in a few seconds a whole new tranche of land on the outside of the town.

As a result of all this devastation, a new town rose from the rubble of old Napier. And because Art Deco was the architectural fashion of the moment, stylised geometric public buildings, offices, banks, shops and houses bloomed like exotic flowers throughout the town. The new buildings were all constructed in reinforced concrete – a material that had proved itself well during the earthquake – which made it easy to create the attractive Deco detailing: sunrises, go-faster stripes, and endless arrangements of geometric shapes such as triangles, diamonds, squares, circles, ovals etc. The fascias could also be rendered with coloured cement plaster, so the buildings are gorgeous mixtures of buff, cream, grey, mint green, mauve, pale blue, yellow, rose, tangerine etc. Every so often you'll see the vivid mauve of a jacaranda tree against a wall of ochre or pale jade: a feast for the eyes (see p12).

I took dozens of photographs of the Deco details on the buildings, and I've designed two quilts for this series inspired by Napier. For this one I concentrated on all those geometric designs and details, using silk dupion in soft mid-pastel colours to reflect the colours of the buildings. I've adapted a basic New York Beauty block for the piecing – hence the name of the quilt – and put it together with a mixture of foundation-piecing and invisible machine appliqué.

Find out more ...

You can discover all kinds of information about Napier's past – and present – at www.artdeconapier.com

---

MAKE YOUR OWN

If you'd like to create your own version of *Napier Beauty*, you'll find the instructions on pages 86-87.

INSIDE INFORMATION

Materials

Silk dupion

Quilting

I added lots of machine-quilting in Deco-style patterns to complement the geometric piecing, using sunrises, waves, spirals, zigzags, triangles and other stylised squiggles. To quilt the ivory-coloured background squares I worked random straight lines in a variegated thread, which unified all the soft colours of the other silks.

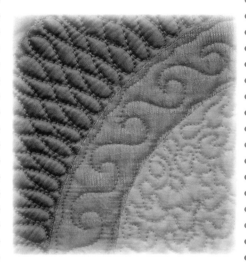

Backing and binding

The plain ivory silk used on the back shows off the quilted designs clearly. For the binding I departed from the plain silks and used a dupion printed with a subtle leaf pattern; the soft shades worked well against all the other colours, and the stylised leaves have a Deco feel themselves.

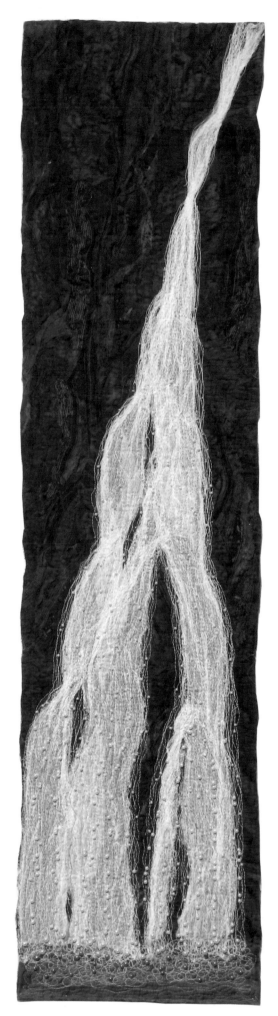

WATERFALL

**A *spectacular torrent thunders down*
*a sheer rock face.***

Water is everywhere in New Zealand. Because it's such a long, thin country, when you fly down it you can quite often see both coasts at the same time (a slight contrast with its nearest neighbour, Australia …), and because there's plenty of coast there are innumerable beaches, inlets, harbours etc. And from the mountains and hills flow equally numberless rivers and streams, producing lakes, deltas, estuaries and – my favourite – waterfalls.

*The waterfall in Napier which
inspired the quilt*

After our first trip to New Zealand several people asked what the highlight was. We enjoyed everything so much, it was hard to pick just one out, but under torture – if, for instance, you tickled my feet or threatened to deprive me of sleep, both of which would make me confess instantly to starting World War Two – I would have to choose several special bush walks. Each of these was uniquely dramatic. Near Kerikeri you can wander beside the river to the Rainbow Falls: as you walk you start to hear the thundering of waters, then, with the noise becoming louder and louder, you reach a clearing where a spectacular waterfall takes your breath away. At Waitangi you can take a boardwalk through magical mangrove swamps to the horseshoe-shaped Haruru Falls. And at the Rapaura Watergardens near Thames, a bush walk takes you from the ornamental gardens through the bush to a ladder of seven waterfalls. And because there are so many sights like this, you often have the whole place to yourself, just to sit and marvel.

So, I had to include a waterfall in my collection, and here it is. Despite its rugged appearance, the particular waterfall that inspired this quilt is actually in the middle of a sedate park in Napier, but none the less spectacular for that.

Rainbow Falls near Kerikeri

Creating realistic-looking water in fabric I think is always a challenge: I decided to use literal veils of fabric to produce the veils of water (see below). The background is a multicoloured sheer print which I manipulated and fused to a bondawebbed foundation fabric; using this technique the print on the sheer fabric became a random pattern suggestive of a cliff face. To create the water I randomly cut several lengths of sheer white crinkled fabric, then twisted it to create the top of the waterfall, where the water appears whiter because it's more concentrated. Then I fanned the fabric out to follow the waterfall shape, cutting sections out of it to allow the 'rock' to show through.

Find out more ...

At www.rapaurawatergardens.co.nz you can take a virtual tour of the gardens, including the waterfall.

THE TECHNIQUE

To enhance the suggestion of water tumbling down the rock face, I added hundreds of pearl bead 'droplets' to the cascade, beginning with tiny ones near the top and working through several sizes to the largest ones at the bottom of the waterfall. In the pool at the bottom I also used some blue beads of the same size to suggest the water being churned up by the torrent. These were all stitched on by hand – and yes, it did take quite a long time!

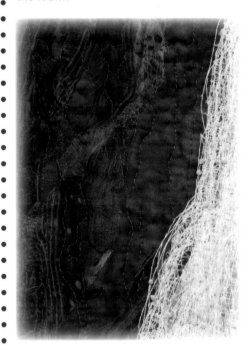

INSIDE INFORMATION

Materials

Cotton and synthetic fabrics, beads

Quilting

I worked the background quilting in long jagged lines to create the impression of the cliff face. The quilting lines on the water did a threefold job, attaching the fabric, quilting the waterfall section and also enhancing the effect of tumbling water. At the bottom of the waterfall I free-machine-quilted swirls in the water to suggest the foam.

Backing and edging

The quilt is backed with a mottled green fabric; I left the edges of the quilt raw to echo the jagged edges of the rock.

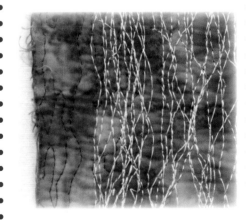

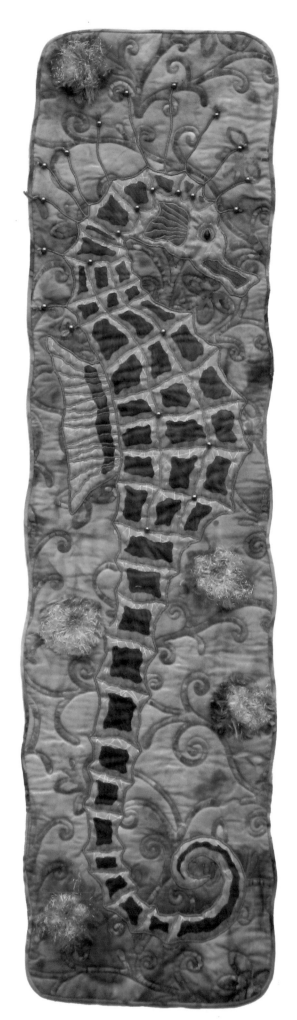

SEAHORSE

A delicate sea-creature looks out shyly from among the fronds of weed.

When I was a child I didn't believe that seahorses actually existed; I'd seen pictures of the strange creatures, with horses' heads and curling tails, and assumed that they were on a par with unicorns and psammeads. Although I know better now, these lovely animals have never lost their magic for me – and if you look at the back cover of this book you'll discover another reason why they're special to us, as they're the logo for our little publishing imprint.

So when we were in Napier it was a given that we'd go and visit Seahorse World, where we saw many thousands of seahorses of various types. (This attraction has actually closed in the past year or two, but there is still an aquarium in Picton where you can view seahorses.) We were mesmerised by the tanks full of magical creatures, all navigating around with flutters of the fins on their backs, or anchoring themselves to strands of seaweed by twining their tails around them.

So, of course, one quilt had to star a seahorse (after all, my chosen format for the quilts seemed custom-built for a seahorse portrait). This individual is having a bit of a bad hair day, but is content because it has a plentiful supply of snacks around it in the form of sea anemones. These serve another purpose too: the rather unusual batik fabric that I wanted to use for the background included butterfly motifs, which didn't seem quite right for under the sea.

Cheerful seahorses form part of a large mural in Napier

A page from my New Zealand scrapbook

So I created five sea anemones from strips of fringed silk and opalescent fabric, which I gathered into tight rings and then appliquéd to cover all the butterflies.

For the fabric that peeps through the different sections of the seahorse's body I used a shaded cotton, which adds richness as the colour gets darker towards the bottom of the shape. Couched threads add texture to the outline and the different lines of the head, embellished with beads around the head sections and scattered across the seahorse's body.

Find out more …

Ecoworld is the new name of what used to be The Seahorse Farm in Picton (www.ecoworldnz.co.nz).

You can also see seahorses at Auckland's Kelly Tarlton's experience, an underground attraction which includes a focus on Antarctic exploration alongside the sea-creature displays (www.kellytarltons.co.nz)

MAKE YOUR OWN

If you'd like to create your own version of *Seahorse*, you'll find the instructions on page 83.

INSIDE INFORMATION

Materials

Print and shaded cotton fabrics, silk and opalescent fabric, coton perlé, beads

Quilting

The seahorse is quilted with the lines of fine satin stitch that decorate its body, gills, nose and fins. The background fronds are outline-quilted by machine, and I used swirls of free machining to both attach and quilt the centres of the sea anemones, leaving the frayed edges to waft in the tide.

Backing and binding

The backing for the design is a layer of plain mauve cotton fabric. To bind the quilt, I cut the edges into random waves and then used the technique described on page 29 (for the Kauri quilt) to add a very narrow binding.

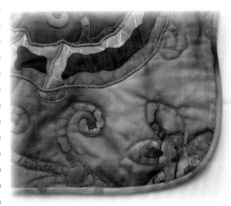

KIWIFRUIT

Of course the land of the kiwi is also the land of the kiwifruit, so I couldn't leave it out of this roll of honour.

As someone else has put it, the best marketing decision the New Zealanders ever made was to change the name of the Chinese Gooseberry (*Actinidia chinensis*, which sounds a little like a fungal infection) to the kiwifruit. The country produces around a quarter of the world's entire crop; in various parts of the north island you can see fields and fields of the vines, propped up on wooden trestles for easier picking (UK strawberry growers take note), surrounded by protective windbreaks of trees or tall bushes. A recent addition to the kiwfruit family is the golden variety, which has less of the sharp tang and a gentler flavour; the usual seed-pattern is there, but the flesh is an attractive gold colour.

Much of the crop is grown around the Bay of Plenty; Te Puke was home to the first NZ kiwfruit vine, planted in 1918, though the first orchard of the fruit wasn't developed until the mid 1930s, by a local grower named Jim McLoughlin. Today Te Puke boasts Kiwifruit Country, a celebration of all aspects of this unique foodstuff; visitors are greeted by a giant emerald-green cross-section of a kiwifruit, and can travel around the plot in a train of small covered carts shaped like cut fruits and towed by a car. I've only seen these in photos, not in the flesh; they're not quite as quaint as the convoy of Cadbury's Creme Egg cars we once saw going down an English motorway, but they're certainly different …

This strange fruit, with its distinctive appearance, has become virtually synonymous with the country as a whole, and crops up everywhere (on T-shirts, keyrings and shopping bags) and in everything (tea, chocolates, local cuisine). I suspect that most of these confections – edible and inedible – are bought by the tourists; the locals probably wouldn't touch them with a bargepole, but they must add considerably to the country's revenue. After the Auckland Symposium in 2005 all the teachers were given the most wonderful package of indigenous goodies, including a bar of kiwifruit soap (made *of* them, not *for* washing them) – dark green, and full of little black seeds. Perfect: a soap with a built-in exfoliant! We even brought

back for friends special spoons designed specifically for scooping out the flesh from the halved fruit. Indeed a national industry.

In my kiwifruit quilt I decided to enlarge the fruit's unmistakable cross-section to a size where it would create its own dramatic piece of abstract art. The different patches of lime green fabric are perfectly set off by the black 'seeds.'

Find out more ...

www.kiwifruitcountry.co.nz

www.zespri.com

THE TECHNIQUE

I decided to use ten different lime (kiwifruit?) greens for the flesh, shading out from the pale centre. I blended the edge of each patch by cutting it into a wiggly line; these lines increase the kind of 'modern abstract' feel of the design. Good old bonding web came to my aid as a method of securing the cut edges; machine stitching would have been too heavy, and would also have been very fiddly round all those wiggles.

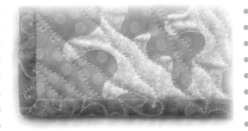

Materials

Black and brown cotton fabrics

Quilting

Once the different layers were bonded in place, I quilted the whole design by machine in a rough grid, using a medium shade of brown which shows up as light on the darkest patches and as dark on the pale areas.

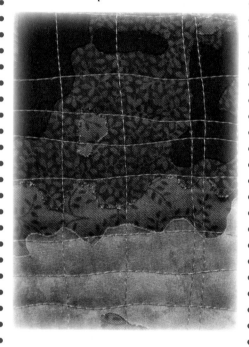

Binding and backing

This design is backed with one of the medium-dark brown fabrics that I'd used in the quilt, and bound with the other.

MOKO

From the shadows the face of a warrior emerges, decorated with traditional tattoo designs.

An image from our evening with the Mitai tribe

Tattoos aren't just the province of disaffected western teenagers; many ancient tribes practised tattooing, and when the Maori came to New Zealand from the Pacific Islands they brought with them the tradition of tattooing their faces and bodies. The Maori facial tattoo, or *moko*, traditionally features stylised elements of their four guardian birds, which include the kiwi (which is a bird but of course doesn't fly), and the bat (OK, they know it's not strictly a bird; but it has got wings, so they consider it an honorary avian).

In Rotorua we went to an evening hosted by the Mitai tribe, and it was a breathtaking experience, introducing us to many aspects of Maori culture (including a truly terrifying *haka*). Following the cultural display we were treated to a *hangi*, food which had been cooking for hours by smoking it in a giant pit lined with heated boulders; it was some of the most delicious food I've ever tasted. Both the men and women of the tribe sported their traditional tattoos; these were painted onto their faces, but only too real on the legs and buttocks of the men – we later saw in Auckland Museum and Te Papa in Wellington some of the implements used to chisel these designs into the skin. After the *hangi* we went for a torchlit walk through the bush to the tribe's own water spring, with the surrounding bush twinkling with the lights from glow-worms, like hundreds of tiny fairy-lights.

It was intriguing to hear how the Maori people are working to keep what is essentially a stone-age culture alive in a modern, forward-thinking country. Through these cultural presentations they involve their young people in the centuries-old traditions such as singing, dancing and games-playing, while also using the most modern techniques to make people aware of what's on

A more contemporary approach: a tattoo parlour in Napier

offer – for instance, this tribe has its own superbly-painted minibuses to ferry tourists to and fro, and the tribal leader at one stage said 'If you'd like to e-mail some photos to your friends, you'll find a computer behind that screen.'

I wanted to celebrate the tradition of the *moko*, but I was also aware that these designs might have special significance to different tribes etc so I didn't want to treat them lightly. I decided to meld the tattoos of various traditions from across the Pacific Islands, blending several modern photographic references with historic drawings of warriors' tattooed faces (including some drawn by Sydney Parkinson, a member of one of Captain Cook's expeditions). The finished design was built up from one black print fabric and three different brown prints, each fabric adding a different depth of colour.

Find out more ...

You'll find many Maori cultural events put on around NZ; to see some lovely images of the tribe which hosted ours, visit www.mitai.co.nz

Te Papa ('Our Place') in Wellington, the official Museum of New Zealand, is a great place for all ages to find out more about the forces that shaped the country; not surprisingly it has a plenty of displays devoted to Maori heritage. www.tepapa.govt.nz

---

THE TECHNIQUE

The final version of the tattooed face was manipulated in Photoshop to create four different levels of colour – originally black, white and two shades of grey. I then enlarged this image enormously and used it to create a kind of 'painting by numbers' drawing, outlining every patch of each of the four shades. Because I wanted my warrior to be in the shadows, I used black plus three shades of brown, rather than using white for the highlights. In the details opposite you can see the four fabrics I picked; each one has a subtle print, giving the finished image more life than if I'd used solid colours.

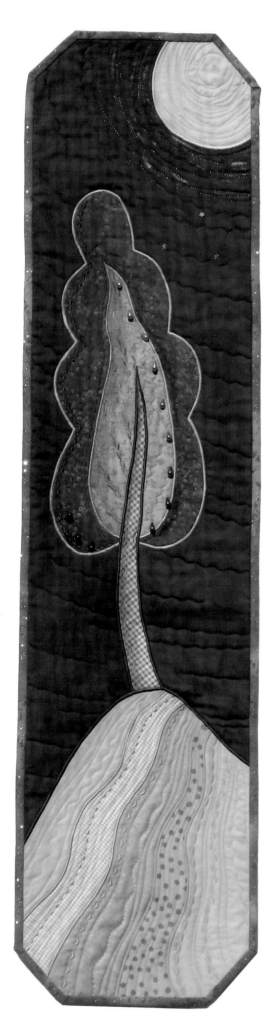

ONE TREE HILL

A dreamy night-time scene, with a fairytale tree at the top of a hill – and could that be a kiwi at its foot?

One unusual aspect of Auckland's landscape is that it's full of verdant green mounds; these are extinct volcanoes, and they pop up round the city's environs like big green puddings. All of them offer spectacular views across the city, and one of the most famous is One Tree Hill, set in Cornwall Park. Cornwall Park was originally a farm owned by Sir John Logan Campbell (1817-1912), one of New Zealand's best-known early settlers who's sometimes known as 'the father of Auckland.' The tent that Campell set up at the bottom of Shortland Street was effectively Auckland's first shop, and he was involved in numerous aspects of New Zealand life including parliament, trading, newspaper publishing, banking and the armed forces. During a royal visit from the Duke and Duchess of Cornwall in 1901, Campell donated his land to the city and it has become a public park – dominated by One Tree Hill in the centre. And in the centre of the hill is an obelisk, marking the tomb of Sir John.

But wait a minute – there isn't a tree on One Tree Hill. Or at least, not at the top. How come? Well, it's a story that began many years ago. In 1640 a tree was planted on its summit, the first in a succession of single trees doomed

The obelisk on One Tree Hill

to violent ends. Perhaps because of the choice of the site (one of the largest prehistoric Maori settlements) for what could be seen as a symbol of colonialism, the unlucky trees on One Tree Hill have been the target of a series of protests, often being cut down as a way of drawing attention to various political and social issues. The most recent tree, a Monterey Pine, was cut down by the council in 2000 (or 2001 or 2002, depending on the source of your information!) as it was unstable after an attack by a Maori wielding a chainsaw (I assume they mean that the tree was physically unstable, but perhaps we can't answer for its emotional state!)

Awesome tree near Kerikeri

It was such a poignant story that I thought I ought to restore a tree to One Tree Hill. As the trees themselves have now passed into legend, I made my tree a kind of fairytale one on a fairytale hill, depicting it at night so that the tree has a dreamlike quality in the moonlight. The background fabric has a subtle damask pattern woven into it, and I added fabric paint to some parts of the design to enrich them. I put the distinctive kite-shaped Southern Cross constellation in the night sky – and as it's night-time, maybe on my dreamtime One Tree Hill the occasional nocturnal kiwi comes out to explore …?

Find out more …

www.aucklandcity.govt.nz/leisure gives you the history of all the city's many different parks

---

MAKE YOUR OWN

If you'd like to create your own version of *One Tree Hill*, you'll find the instructions on page 88.

INSIDE INFORMATION

Materials

Cotton plain, print and damask fabrics, fabric paint, beads

Quilting

The sky behind the tree is quilted in random wavy lines in navy blue, then I've enhanced these with lines of gold outside the moon. The tree itself and the hills are quilted with lines of machine stitching using plain and fancy stitches.

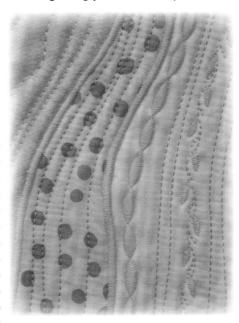

Backing and binding

The backing fabric is plain pale blue. To bind the edges I wanted something with a little fairytale sparkle, so picked out this deep gold marbed cotton fabric with a shimmery finish. The corners are trimmed at 45° to soften the right angles.

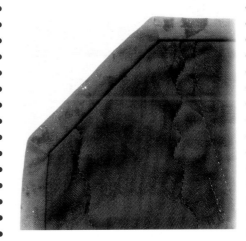

ROTORUA

A trip to Rotorua is an unforgettable experience –
not least for all the bright mineral pools with
their encrustations of colourful crystals.

When we first knew that we would be visiting New Zealand, one of the places we knew we had to visit was Rotorua. Notwithstanding the Rolf Harris song of 1968, the place had always had a magical sound, and we wanted to see the mineral pools and the hot and cold geysers. Various people advised us not to spend too many nights there, as the smell can be overwhelming, so we booked into a B&B for two nights. The cheery Yorkshireman who owned the B&B came to pick us up from the coach station; he and his wife had emigrated 40-odd years previously and hadn't lost an ounce of their native accent. Without the slightest trace of a Kiwi twang he was chatting away: 'Me and the waaaf, we doon't nootice the smell, but ah expect you can smell t' soolfer, caan't you?' As we sat with hands over mouths and noses, all we could do was nod …

There's no getting away from it, Rotorua certainly can smell, but it isn't always overwhelming; it goes in waves, and in some parts of the area you don't notice it at all. It's the only golf course I've ever seen where the sand hazards have fumaroles coming out of them. And the mineral pools and geysers are breathtaking; for countless years the waters have been bubbling up from the deep, bringing various minerals; these minerals crystallise as they concentrate in certain areas, and dry out into coloured crusts, combining in an endless array of vivid colours – in fact one pool is called the Artist's Palette. And some of them are almost unbelievable colours; do you remember Instant Whip? (The forerunner of Angel Delight, for those people a bit younger than me.) Remember the lime-flavoured one? Well, one of the pools in Rotorua looked exactly as though it was full of lime Instant Whip: opaque, and the most extraordinary shade of luminous green.

Of course I had to try and paint my own version of these sights; I tried to capture some of the glorious colours and textures of these layers of encrustation.

I began with a fabric which had been folded and random-dyed so that it came out in rough stripes of bright colour; this gave me my base palette, which I then enhanced and embellished. I added insertions of gathered silk (see below), and layered randomly-cut strips of sheer

fabrics in different colours and textures to create depth: I then added thicker textures with beads and embroidery.

Find out more ...

www.geyserland.co.nz is the website of Wai-O-Tapu thermal park, the area near Rotorua which includes most of the geysers and geothermal pools

Nikki Tinkler's book *Quilting with a Difference* (published by P&Q, ISBN 1 900371 70 7) has lots of ideas on using embroidery stitches for quilting

---

THE TECHNIQUE

To create silk insertions, I first cut random wedge shapes in the cotton background. For each one I then cut a larger wedge-shaped piece of silk dupion in a toning colour, and ran gathering threads down each long edge. When I pulled up the gathering threads I kept the gathers as uneven as possible to create a textured triangle; I then fitted the gathered shape behind the gap in the cotton fabric, pinned the layers together, and stitched by machine down the cut edges of the background fabric to hold the silk in place.

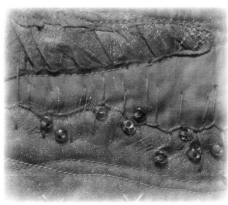

GREEN-LIPPED MUSSELS

A New Zealand speciality, the wonderfully-named bivalve is at home in its marine surroundings.

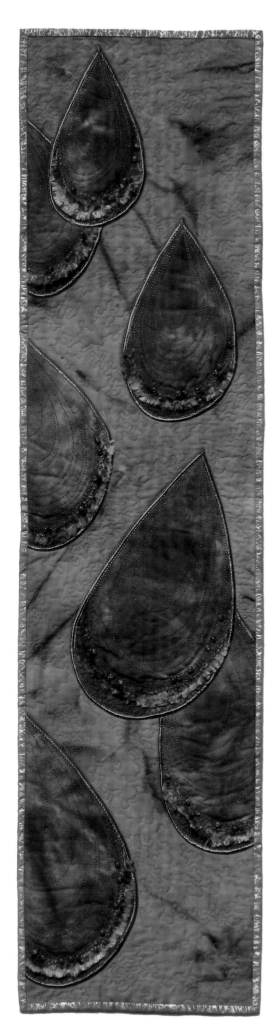

The fish and seafood is one of the many things that we enjoyed in New Zealand – an all-time highlight would have to be sitting on the beach at Napier, looking out over the vast expanse of Hawke's Bay, eating deep-friend scallops with kumara (sweet potato) chips which had cost the equivalent of about £1.25p. The green-lipped mussel is a meaty (?!) seafood delicacy often found on menus; you can even buy them from supermarkets. They sit in their glass tanks glopping happily at passersby, presumably not realising that the person pointing enthusiastically into the tank isn't an impressed admirer, but their nemesis looking for tonight's supper. Havelock, according to the Dorling Kindersley *Eyewitness Guide*, is 'the self-styled green lip mussel capital of the world;' cultivating the shellfish is one of Havelock's main industries, but you can find them in plenty of other places too.

These glamorous shellfish have also become popular in recent years as they've been found to have anti-

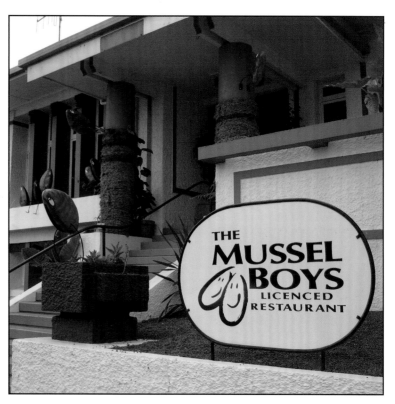

inflammatory properties; health-food websites are full of green-lipped mussel extracts in various forms. I decided to feature my mussels in a slightly more glamorous setting than a supermarket tank or a chemist's bottle; here they are in their underwater habitat, getting together perhaps for a green-lipped mussel family reunion. The shells are actually quite large, but my versions are even larger than life. I created the padded shell shapes (see below) individually, working in a deep aquamarine hand-dyed fabric, then zigzagged these to the background fabric. I embellished the 'beards' of the shells with fringes of variegated textured knitting yarn, and used the stained glass patchwork technique to edge them with metallic bias binding. Green beads added the final texture.

Find out more …

If you're travelling to New Zealand and are interested in trying out the good old green-lip (or some of its other relations), The Mussel Boys (see photographs!) is a franchise. Tap 'Mussel Boys New Zealand' into your search engine, and you'll discover the location of the different outlets.

THE TECHNIQUE

In order to give the shells extra dimension I used the goldwork technique of building up layers of padding (in this case, wadding). For each shell I cut its shape in wadding and then cut a series of further shapes, each one slightly smaller. I then piled these up in order with the largest on top to create a mussel-shaped dome; piling them up in this way gives you a smoothly-domed shape and prevents the stepped appearance you'd get if you piled them up from large to small. I laid the top fabric over this pile of shapes and machine-quilted the lines on the shells to stabilise the padded layers.

INSIDE INFORMATION

Materials

Cotton fabrics, synthetic yarn, metallic bias binding, beads

Quilting

For the background I wanted to suggest seawater without either depicting waves or stipple-quilting the fabric to death, so I did a variation of stipple-quilting (or vermicelli). I stitched small patches with quite fine conventional vermicelli quilting, then meandered the line in long squiggles across the plain areas to work another patch of vermicelli. This created a random background which is much more suggestive of water than if I'd worked the same texture across the whole quilt.

Backing and binding

The backing is another piece of mottled green fabric; for the binding I used a jade green and gold print cotton, which picked up the gleam of the beads and the metallic binding without being too glitzy.

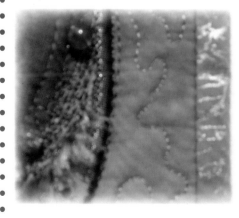

INSIDE INFORMATION

Materials

Cotton fabrics, lace, fusible interfacing

Quilting

The background is quilted by machine in random swirls to suggest the cream and meringue, and the machine satin stitch round the appliquéd shapes also quilts the design. The fruit pieces are quilted individually in suitable patterns.

Backing and binding

The backing is a plain piece of cream fabric; for the binding I used strips of fabric printed with various little fruits on a cream background.

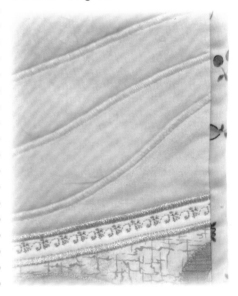

PAVLOVA

***Anyone for Christmas pudding? This is it –
Kiwi-style!***

The Ozzies and the Kiwis have ongoing rivalries in many areas of life – not least sport, but in many other aspects of life too. (Although, as Bill Bryson points out, Australia wins hands down on the number of animals per square metre who are out to get you. New Zealand has only one poisonous spider – I presume by this that they mean one species, rather than one individual …) Everywhere, you come across this rivalry: whose beaches are best, whose climate is best, whose steaks/beers/girls/ cricketers are best. At the Maori evening we went to, a small irrepressible Ozzie boy piped up 'Did you really used to eat people?' To which the answer, quick as a flash, was 'Yes – but only Australians.'

But surely one of the strangest fields of rivalry is not nearly so macho: who invented the pavlova. I'm not kidding: emotions run high on this touchy subject, with each country laying claim to the delicious dessert. Claims and counter-claims cross the Tasman sea with the regularity of Posh Spice changing her hairstyle. Personally, I don't care who invented it, as long as someone did! When I asked what most New Zealanders eat for Christmas dinner the answer I got was 'Pavlova.' (I was really wondering what takes the place of our terminally dull turkey, but perhaps pavlova counts as the centrepiece of the feast.) Just in case there's anyone out there in some far-flung outpost that pavlova hasn't reached, it's a confection of meringue, cream and fresh fruit, and is a great showcase for all the fresh fruit grown all over the country – not just kiwifruit, but cherries, peaches, raspberries etc.

We did our bit for the entente cordiale by trying as many different pavlovas as possible (including on Christmas Day), so it seemed only fitting to honour New Zealand's (or is it Australia's?) national pudding with its own quilt. A section down a pavlova seemed the obvious way to go, so I've arranged my dessert on a plate (decorated with a Maori-inspired border design, and a lacy embossed edging) and topped it with fresh fruit. A white-on-white cotton fabric became the cream, and a mottled beige batik was ideal meringue fabric. To make the piped rosettes of cream and meringue extra-dimensional, I cut wadding patches in the same shapes and positioned them behind the appropriate areas. When I stitched through all the layers by machine (carefully, as by then the quilt was quite thick) it made the rosettes look heavily sculpted.

Find out more ...

If you want to see how high emotions run on the pavlova debate, tap 'who invented pavlova?' into your internet search engine. The results will give you both sides of the argument, as well as pointing you in the direction of various pavlova recipes.

THE TECHNIQUE

The appliqué fruit pieces are made from fusible interfacing (try Fast2Fuse or FlexiFirm), sandwiched between layers of cotton fabric. I traced the shapes onto the covered interfacing, then quilted them by machine with appropriate textures; once they were quilted I cut out the shapes and edged them with machine satin stitch. To add a little dimension to the grapes I added a highlight in pale fabric crayon to each one. If you feel the urge to add your own fruit salad to a quilted project, you'll find the full-size templates for the different fruit shapes on page 93.

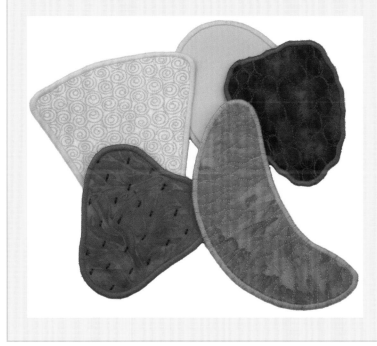

TANIKO

A woven quilt uses an enlarged version of a traditional Maori weaving design.

Some of the most iconic plants of the country are the New Zealand Flaxes (*phormiums*); their large spiky leaves, which look rather like our yucca, appear everywhere in the countryside, topped with delicate fronds of flowers (see p26). These flaxes are very important in traditional Maori life; war canoes and buildings were held together with twisted flax cords, and the green leaves are scraped and allowed to curl into tubes, then threaded to create the classic striped 'grass' skirts. Flax weaving is a traditional Maori skill; green leaves could be woven quickly to create temporary platters and carrying baskets, and more long-lasting items are made by soaking and then stripping the leaves and drying the strips. Woven flax panels can often be seen in meeting houses, and the skill is also used to create ceremonial cloaks, and the classic Maori *kete*, or woven bag. The weaving designs can be very intricate, sometimes using reeds interspersed with the flax for contrast.

Maori woodcarving showing New Zealand flax plants

For my design (which I've given the name of one of the Maori weaving traditions) I've used a characteristic pattern; I've created it with strips of ivory-coloured fabric to suggest the flax, woven with thinner strips of red-brown ribbon to suggest thinner contrast strips of reed. The original design makes use of long vertical strips of flax in pairs: I used double-width tubes of fabric, padded with wadding then stitched down the centre to create two bands. The ribbons are woven over and under the strips in groups of three; if you look carefully you can see how the design works, with each trio of ribbons going over one double 'flax' band then behind three more.

Tucked into the weaving is a typical Maori greenstone fishhook design – these stylised versions of practical objects were presumably carved originally to celebrate the importance of a good fishhook in making the difference between a good meal and going to bed hungry. The greenstone (nephrite jade, or *pounamu*) is itself of great practical and spiritual significance to the Maori; it was the hardest material known to the ancient tribes, and was used for

A little Maori-style basket woven by Jenny Papa

making tools, weapons and jewellery, each one being painstakingly shaped by many hours of sanding. The greenstone is found in West Coast rivers, where the boulders have been flushed out of their seams in the mountains by erosion; in 1997 a special settlement handed the rights to the West Coast greenstone back to the Ngai Tahu tribe of the south island. Stylised fishhook shapes are still favourite NZ souvenirs, some carved from greenstone, others from cheaper bone, and the beautiful flowing shapes are also often immortalised in other arts and crafts such as woodcarving and painting.

Find out more ...

www.aotearoa.co.nz/flaxworks will give you some beautiful examples of Maori weaving, and www.catrina. co.nz is the website of Catrina Sutter, who does contemporary weaving in the Maori style

To see some examples of carved greenstone pendants, go to www.nzpacific.com/Maori-Jewelry

If you'd like to plant some New Zealand flaxes in your garden (as we've recently done!), you'll find a good selection at www.south-west-phormiums.co.uk

THE TECHNIQUE

I found an unusual print fabric in my mother's stash; it looks rather like malachite, so seemed a good choice for a greenstone fishhook motif. I used machine cutwork for the shape, fusing the fabric first of all onto each side of a piece of double-sided fusible interfacing; I then cut out the shape and edged it with machine satin stitch.

INSIDE INFORMATION

Materials
Mottled and print cotton fabrics, ribbon

Quilting
Each large strip is quilted down the centre, then once I'd woven the design and pinned the ribbons in place I added the backing and used a decorative machine stitch to secure the ribbons. Stitching through all the layers in this way anchored the woven design securely.

Backing and binding
The swirly print on the backing fabric has echoes of Maori koru curls or spirals, and the natural colours complement the fabrics of the weaving itself; I brought the fabric over the edges of the quilt to create the binding as well.

WAYSIDE FLOWERS

Bright blooms created from lace motifs decorate a background of layered sheers.

Something you can't help noticing in the top of the north island is the flowers that grow by the side of the road. Because of the subtropical climate and fertile soil, flowers of all kinds grow abundantly along the kerbside: giant agapanthus in mauve and white, montbretia, deep purple and pink convolvulus, classy daisies, and the most vivid hydrangeas I've ever seen. The effect is even more striking if you visit in their summer/our winter, when roadsides at home are often acres of dismal grey slush.

I never tired of seeing these kerbside flowers as we travelled around (and I couldn't stop photographing them, either …), so I knew I had to represent them in one of the quilts. It's a rather nice concept, really: ephemeral flowers (convolvulus aren't called 'Morning Glory' for nothing) being immortalised in a quilt. I built the background by layering squares and rectangles of bright sheer fabrics over a piece of vivid green silk dupion; where the sheers overlapped this created lots of secondary and tertiary colours and shades, which gave the background

added depth. I also found a very attractive green lacy fabric which included metallic threads; this created an illusion of foliage when I added it to the sheer layers.

I used lines of machine quilting in different colours and stitch patterns to suggest the different leaves and stems, then on top I used flower motifs cut from guipure lace. For the white agapanthus I left them virgin, but painted some to create the purple flowerheads. For the montbretia blossoms I painted smaller guipure flowers in shades of red and orange and arranged them along branching stems. The convolvulus were made from layers of different bright sheers, which produced a really deep, rich colour, and the hydrangea blossoms were again white or painted guipure motifs.

Find out more ...

www.edengarden.co.nz was one of our favourite gardens

THE TECHNIQUE

Many guipure laces include flower or leaf motifs, and it's fun to cut these out and reorder them into your own flower arrangements. I coloured mine using various fabric paints which I set by ironing the dry motifs. During this process I discovered that not all guipure lace is made of cotton – some is made of polyester, which melts dramatically! I overcame this problem (once I'd picked the caramelised flowers off the soleplate of my iron ...) by using a non-stick ironing sheet between the motifs and the iron.

Materials

Silk dupion, sheer and lacy synthetic fabrics, guipure lace motifs

Quilting

I suggested the shapes of the agapanthus heads with radiating lines of machine quilting, and used an automatic machine stitch for the stems of the montbretia. I wanted to include spiky leaves for the montbretia but didn't want them to dominate the other shapes, so I drew them in with overlapping wiggles of free machining. Once all the lace flower motifs were in place I stitched leaf designs into the background with free machine quilting.

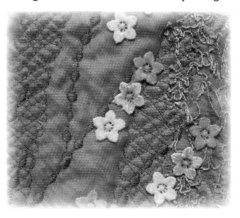

Backing and binding

The back of the quilt is a second piece of the shot green silk; as I'd left the edges of the sheer patches raw on the quilt top, I felt it would be most appropriate to leave the edges of the quilt unbound too. So the edges are simply sealed with a fairly large zigzag to keep the wadding hidden and to prevent the silk from fraying too much; the turquoise and green warp and weft threads of the shot silk show at the edges as fringes.

A IS FOR APPLE

The samplers stitched by long-ago schoolgirls echo down the centuries.

My favourite apples are Braeburns. This might sound like an odd comment, but bear with me. The first Braeburn, we were reliably informed, was a self-seeded hybrid ('mutant' sounds a bit rude for such a lovely fruit), found growing on a fruit farm in the north island. The farseeing farmer recognised a stranger in the orchard, as it were, but allowed it to grow and bear fruit. And so the first Braeburns – for such they were – were born. So every Braeburn ever produced since is the spiritual love-child of that illicit tryst – not a literal offspring in the sense of being from the same original tree (it's hard to get away from Adam-and-Eve-type imagery here), but the product of a similar hybrid.

I wanted to feature a Braeburn on one of my quilts, and decided to use it to bring together several other ideas. If you go to Kerikeri you can see the three oldest buildings in New Zealand (obviously built for their handy proximity to the airport …) – and yet they only date back to the 1820s

The Stone Store at Kerikeri

or so. In this era schoolchildren in New Zealand, as in the UK – particularly little girls – were being taught all the useful skills that would see them through life, and most of the girls would have produced cross-stitch samplers. These often included little gnomic sayings or proverbs, or featured lists such as A is for Apple, B is for Ball, C is for Cat etc. So I've made my own alphabet sampler in honour of the Braeburn.

At the top of the design is a picture of the Stone Store, the country's oldest surviving stone building. This was built in 1835 and began life as a storehouse, fortified with stone to protect the precious goods inside; it gradually transmogrified into a shop, and is now a souvenir shop and museum. I don't know if it has (or had) an apple tree in the garden, but I've given it one. I've also included several cross-stitched bands with the beginning of my Apple Alphabet: moving from the top of the quilt to the bottom, they say:

A is for Apple (with a juicy red apple at each end of the band)

B is for Braeburn

C is for Crunchy (the apples seem to have been slightly munched here …)

Apple sculpture on the shore at Wellington

D is for Delicious

E is for Eaten (the apples are now reduced just to cores).

I've incorporated all the bands (including one that's just a row of rosy apples) into a crazy patchwork sampler, featuring lots of traditional plaids and prints and embellished with country-style buttons and beads. If you fancy producing an old-fashioned alphabet sampler, you'll find a chart for all the letters (and the apples!) on page 87.

Find out more …

www.teara.govt.nz is the online New Zealand encyclopedia; on it you'll find entries for 'pipfruit in New Zealand' (which will tell you all about the various apples and pears grown), and for Kerikeri, which will give you the history of the area around the Stone Store.

THE TECHNIQUE

To assemble the sampler itself I used crazy stained glass patchwork, cutting the fabric patches to shape and then sealing the raw edges under strips of ribbon, cream broderie anglaise and lace, coloured ricrac and my cross-stitched bands. The wavy shape around the outside is a good counterpoint to all the straight internal lines; I appliquéd the curved shape to the apple-print background with a small zigzag, then covered the zigzag with cream flowered lace.

INSIDE INFORMATION

Materials

Cotton fabrics, embroidered Aida fabric and bands, lace, ribbons and ribbon bows, ricrac, broderie anglaise, buttons and beads

Quilting

I used the buttons and ribbon bows to quilt the work, stitching through all the layers as I attached them.

Backing and binding

The backing and binding are done with one piece of fabric; I chose a blue-and-white print which features little berries, and brought the edges of the fabric to the front of the quilt to bind the raw edges.

Materials

Mottled and print cottons, fusible bias binding

Quilting

To echo the strong lines of the design I outlined each patch with big-stitch quilting in black coton à broder. To create coloured details I scattered seeding stitches across the individual 'claws' of the flowers, using lime-green coton à broder on the yellow patches, and variegated orange/red/yellow thread on the red areas.

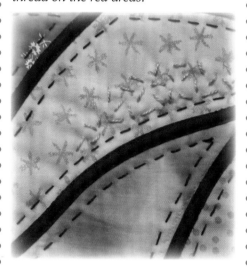

Backing

The bright print fabric I used for the back picks up all the different colours of the quilt front.

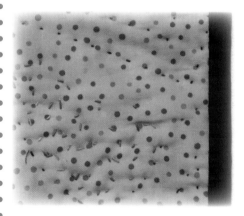

Binding

The binding is plain black cotton, to continue the dramatic lines of the bias binding and the black stitching.

HELICONIA

The absurb bloom of the heliconia plant is framed against a background of verdant foliage.

Because the far north of New Zealand is subtropical, all kinds of tropical flowers grow wild in the bush: walking through the bush paths we came across pink (and standard) passionflowers and wild jasmine, for instance. And the botanic gardens offer even more exotic blooms: this spectacular heliconia, or lobster-claw plant (you can see where it gets its name) was in the Auckland Winter Gardens, a series of glasshouses which form part of the Auckland Domain (a large public park created on land which was set aside for the purpose as long ago as 1840).

It was such a dramatic flower, it deserved a dramatic quilt, so I created it in stained glass patchwork in a selection of bright citrus colours. The shapes are so extraordinary that I decided to use the Rayonnist technique of extending the

main lines of the design across the background – this also then handily breaks the background into patches ready for appliquéing in different fabrics. I decided to give the quilt a slightly folky feel (don't ask me why – I can't remember), so I picked print fabrics in bright colours, complemented by a few mottled cottons.

Find out more ...

There are various guides to the flora of New Zealand; one of the most accessible versions is the Wikipedia entry!

MAKE YOUR OWN

If you'd like to create your own version of *Heliconia*, you'll find the instructions on page 89.

GOLD

The promise of gold brought many people to New Zealand – but their lives weren't always easy ...

Many different things brought the founders of New Zealand to the country and encouraged them to stay. For the Maori, land and space were important. Timber was a great attraction, and so was the kauri gum that could be dug out of the ancient forests (see p28). Many people came simply for a new life (see p24), believing that the promise of the new world could not be

Above: Tony Stones' sculpture of a settler family, on the Nelson seafront

Right: the old wharf at Thames

worse than the realities of the old. But one of the most persuasive lures was that ancient love: gold. By strange coincidence, the ancestor of one of our friends, a Mr Charles Ring, was the first person to find gold in New Zealand (in 1852), and there is still a road named after him in the area. In 1861 prospector Gabriel Read discovered gold in Gabriel's Gully (about 60 miles west of Dunedin), and so began the Otago Gold Rush, which brought many thousands of people to the area. Attention then moved to the wild west coast of the south island, where other discoveries had been made. Around all of these areas you will still find various exhibitions, displays and even whole ghost towns associated with the gold industry. There's still one gold mine in New Zealand, the open pit at Waihi, which reopened after the discovery of new seams.

The gold prospectors, of course, had mixed fortunes. Many of the people who flocked to the Cormandel peninsula discovered that much of the gold in that area was embedded in quartz, and difficult and expensive to extract. That didn't stop them, though, from staking their claims and mining the unforgiving rock – and some people's seams produced eye-wateringly valuable yields of gold. (Think how infuriating it must have been if your claim was for the next bit of rock along!) The population of nearby Thames swelled to 18,000 (it's currently less than 7,000), and we saw photographs showing hundreds of squalid huts crammed together, as people lived cheek by jowl, raising their families and trying to keep body and soul alive as they sought their fortune.

I was intrigued by the idea of all these different people who had been drawn to the country for different reasons, and became the ancestors of the modern-day New Zealanders. I wanted to do a quilt which in some way honoured these people who sometimes had travelled half-way round the world in difficult conditions in order to (sometimes literally) carve out a living in often even more hostile conditions. The dark, rough background of this quilt represents that hardship – with the streak of elusive gold down the middle.

I managed to track down some ships' rosters for early settlers, and incorporated some of the details into this quilt; it was amazing to think that, back in the mid 19th century, these were real people coming to the country for a new life. The *Caroline*, which sailed from Melbourne in 1834, described its passengers as all being gold-diggers. Some of the details are terribly poignant – for instance: '*Commodore Perry*, departed Liverpool, Victoria 5th September 1860. Mrs E L Deane 27; Georgina Deane 3; Stanley Deane 1 died on voyage; Sydney Deane 2 died on voyage.' And yet there are also some lovely vignettes: the *Abbey*, which also sailed out of Melbourne in 1855, lists several passengers whose occupations are given as 'Musician.' It's a great picture, to think that at the end of a week's hard work, people would gather at a local hostelry; someone would strike up a tune from the old country, and for a few hours the cares of the day could be forgotten.

Find out more ...

www.goldmine-experience.co.nz

THE TECHNIQUE

I typed the details from the ships' rosters in a style similar to the official lists of the time (being married to a typographer, I wanted to give them the most authentic look possible!), then darkened the background and printed the lists out on fabric. As I incorporated them into the quilt I added a layer of netting over the top of each one – I wanted to suggest the idea that although these names have almost vanished into the mists of time, yet they were real people who all played their part in establishing the country of New Zealand.

INSIDE INFORMATION

Materials

Synthetic fabrics, corduroy, felt, velvet, imitation suede, net, cotton fabric, gold ribbon

Quilting

I built the layers of the quilt up with random shapes cut from thick fabrics with a soldering iron (see p29), so any detailed quilting would have got lost in the pile of the fabrics. Instead I worked machine quilting in random lines from the top to the bottom of the quilt, stitched so that the lines overlap in places.

Backing and edging

I wanted to leave the edges of this quilt raw, to tie in with the rough background texture; for the wadding I used a layer of brown felt so that it would blend. The backing fabric is a woodgrain print, which I chose to echo the wood of the ships used to bring the settlers from far-off lands.

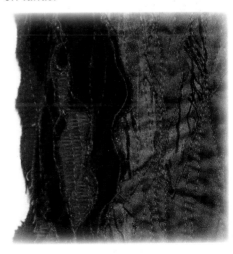

Materials

Plain and shaded cotton fabrics

Quilting

I quilted the fins and tail heavily with lines of machine stitching, then continued these in variegated thread along the body at random intervals, echoing the slightly wavy lines of the woven shapes. A bit of vermicelli/stipple quilting on the head adds texture, and free-machined round the fish's spots and his eye to secure the patches and to add decoration.

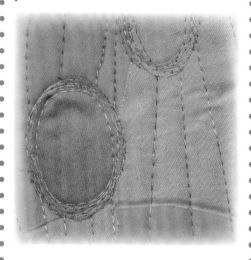

Backing and edging

The backing for the fish is a layer of plain cream cotton fabric. To seal the layers of the quilt sandwich I stitched around the outline of the fish with a small zigzag, then cut away the excess fabric with sharp scissors; I then finished off the edges of all the head, tail, fins and body with lines of machine satin stitch in toning colours, supported by a layer of tearaway foundation fabric.

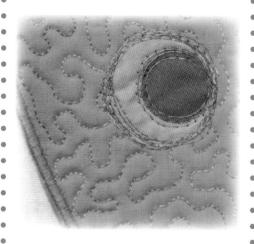

FISH

The smile on the face of this fish suggests that it's the one that got away …

As lovers of fish and seafood we relished the bounty of the seas on offer in New Zealand restaurants (see also page 46), and tried several new types of fish during our visits. Fish and chips is as popular there as it is at home – although theirs is quite often a healthier version, perhaps rolled in oats and quickly fried, or served grilled with kumara (sweet potato) chips. The pronunciation takes a little while to get used to: Joe Bennett in his book *A Land of Two Halves* talks about New Zealanders moving all their vowels around one position, so that (for instance) 'fish and chips' becomes 'fush and chups;' we actually saw it written that way on one menu board, so it's obviously something that even the Kiwis are aware of!

One time I saw 'Fish in a Bowl' on a drinks menu, and had to order one just so that I could see what it was – I had visions of slurping slightly seaweedy water out of a goldfish bowl while trying to ensure that I didn't get a small guppy up my nose. The actuality turned out to be more appetising, and still quite imaginative: chocolate fish (a favourite Kiwi sweet treat – marshmallow shapes covered in chocolate) floating/melting into an interesting pink goo in a large cup of milky coffee, with another pristine chocolate fish on the side (presumably for dunking?). I was never quite brave enough to order a 'Fluffy', another star of the drinks menu – maybe that was one of the much-hated possums (unwelcome migrants

from Oz which are voracious consumers of New Zealand bush) – floating face down in a cup of mocha? (During our second trip I discovered what a Fluffy is, but I won't spoil the surprise by telling you if you don't already know.)

Anyway, I digress …I obviously had to immortalise a fish in one of my quilts, but it was difficult to know precisely which one to pick. It seemed best, eventually, to do a kind of generic fish: let one stand for all. And judging by the happy smile on its face, it's pleased to have its portrait in a book. This is my first woven quilt; I'd seen the technique used on several quilts to good effect, and thought I'd have a go. I used shaded fabrics for the weaving, to add extra dimension to the interlocking areas.

Find out more …

Joe Bennett's book *A Land of Two Halves: An Accidental Tour of New Zealand* is a sardonic but affectionate personal portrait of New Zealand; the author is British by birth, but has lived in NZ for 17 years and writes a regular column for the one of the country's newspapers. The book is published by Scribner, ISBN 978-0743263573.

If you'd like to see more New Zealand sealife, the national aquarium is on the seafront at Napier (www.nationalaquarium.co.nz).

And if you fancy trying more woven quilt designs, check out *Simply Stunning Woven Quilts* by Anna Faustino, published by C&T, ISBN 9781571204523

MAKE YOUR OWN
If you'd like to create your own version of *Fish*, you'll find the instructions on page 90.

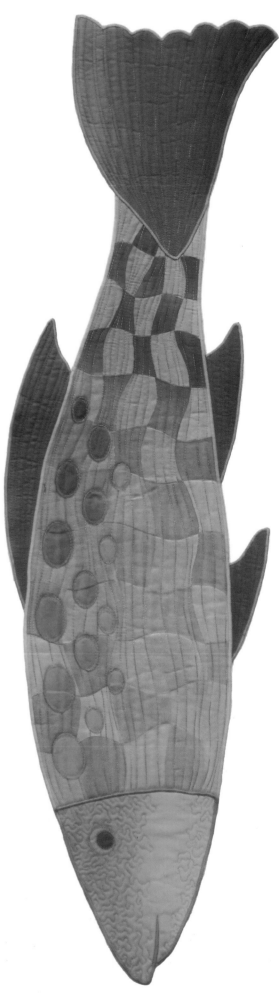

BUSH FERN

The green fronds of a fern curl across a background of batik vegetation.

Ferns, of course, are inseparable from New Zealand; if you're a rugby fan you'll know that the silver fern – the national plant – is the emblem of the All Blacks, and ferns of all kinds cover the islands both in actuality and in symbol. A significant proportion of the remaining native bush is formed from different kinds of fern, and cultivated species fill gardens; as well as the real thing, stylised forms of the open fronds and the fiddlehead-shaped young sprouts (think bracken) decorate logos, telephone boxes, carvings and paintings. When we spent the evening learning about the Maori Mitai tribe (see p40) we finished off the evening walking through the bush and learning about the different uses of various ferns, and since I've been home I've read an article about Charles Royal, who is using native New Zealand plants – including ferns – in recipes.

We visited a garden that apparently included an example of every different kind of fern in New Zealand (I have to be honest and say that, as a non-botanist, most of them looked pretty much the same to me), but nothing beats walking among them in the bush, smelling the wild jasmine and listening to the sounds of the birds and insects. At these times you get a glimpse of what it must have been like for the early white settlers, hacking paths through this densely-packed bush with all its exotic species, many of which were unknown in their homelands.

Not surprising, then, that ferns crop up quite often in my collection of New Zealand quilts (see pages 6, 26 and 64) – and this bush fern is one incarnation. In it I'm trying to convey the sense of the vegetation in the bush – a tumble of

Neil Dawson's fern sphere hangs over Wellington's Civic Square

deep greens, but in many different patterns and textures. I decided to do this with a traditional Log Cabin block, but pieced throughout in green batik fabrics featuring ferns, leaves and fronds. On top of the pieced background I've embroidered a single proud fern in feather stitch (I probably should have used fern stitch, but I prefer the look of feather stitch!), working in a variegated thread.

Find out more …

www.maorifood.com will introduce you to the work of Charles Royal and his recipes

---

MAKE YOUR OWN

If you'd like to create your own version of *Bush Fern* you'll find the instructions on page 92-93.

INSIDE INFORMATION

Materials

Print and batik cotton fabrics

Quilting

The quilting is done with the embroidered fern – the feather stitch is worked through all the layers to create a decorative quilted design.

Backing

Another classic native fabric; I've got a piece of this same print with a white background, too.

Binding

For the binding I found yet another green batik that I hadn't included in the piecing, which meant that, while blending with all the other fabrics in colour, it was still visible against them all.

DECO FERN

Stylised foliage designs inspired by the 1930s create a very different fern quilt.

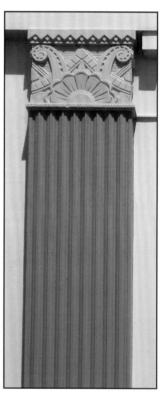

$\mathcal{A}$s well as the strongly geometric patterns beloved of the Art Deco designers (see p32), stylised plant designs – flowers, leaves, ferns, stems, trees etc – were also very popular, and so also appear on the buildings in Napier and its surrounding towns. These designs were heavily influenced by the Mayan and Inca/Aztec motifs of central America, which were often created in simple relief in stone or clay; the two-dimensional nature of the motifs complemented the more mathematical aspects of Deco design. As ferns are such a large part of New Zealand identity (see p6), a stylised Mayan-style fern seemed too good to miss.

Another aspect of Napier's proud 30s heritage is the Art Deco Weekend. Despite a few disasters in the 1980s when some of the classic buildings were knocked down, the citizens of Napier are well aware of the gem they possess, and they work hard to conserve the special nature of the town. Every year, on the third weekend in February, people flock there dressed in 1930s fashions and driving contemporaneous cars, and the weekend finishes with the

Gatsby Picnic in the seaside Marine Parade Gardens. If you're visiting in late July, you can take part in Deco Decanted, a smaller version of the February celebration. And when we were there it was possible to book a vintage car tour, with the  blazer-and-boater-clad Bertie taking people on a tour of Napier's highlights in his 1934 Buick.

Deco dresses used all kinds of sumptuous fabrics, so I decided to do the same on my *Deco Fern*; many of the fabrics are silk, including some beautiful woven silk brocades. I picked a colour palette featuring shades of tangerine, lime and lemon – all colours popular at the time – and I used gold bias binding to reflect the idea of what were sometimes called the *jeunesse d'orée*, the 'golden young people' or 'bright young things' of the age. The quilt is created in stained glass patchwork, and I've embellished it with deco-style beads in toning colours.

Find out more ...

As well as the sites which will tell you about the Deco activities in Napier (eg www.artdeconapier.com), try www.artdeco.org.nz, which is the website of the Auckland Art Deco Society. Ranfurly, near Queenstown, has its own annual Art Deco festival, celebrating its 44 Deco buildings.

MAKE YOUR OWN

If you'd like to create your own version of *Deco Fern*, you'll find the instructions on page 91.

INSIDE INFORMATION

Materials

Plain and embroidered silk dupions and brocades, cotton fabric, beads, fusible bias binding

Quilting

The strong lines of the design are echoed by lines of machine stitching in Deco patterns such as triangles, leaves and Egyptian key designs – the Deco designers were heavily influenced by the discovery of Tutankhamen's tomb in 1922, with all its stylised motifs. I used these lines to quilt the piece as well as to embellish it.

Backing and binding

The backing and binding are done with one piece of fabric; I chose a mottled cotton print in a dark shade of tangerine, and brought the edges of the fabric to the front of the quilt to bind the raw edges.

Materials

Cotton fabric, assorted fabric paints, beads, jewels (fake …)

Quilting

I quilted the feather shape intensively to give the impression of all the individual fronds, just using straight machine stitch and a walking foot.

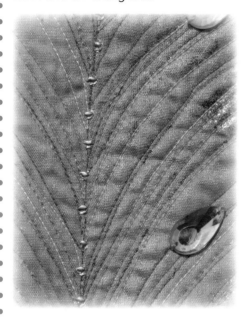

Backing and edging

The backing for the feather is a layer of plain pink cotton fabric. To seal the layers of the quilt sandwich I stitched around the outline of the feather with a small zigzag, then cut away the excess fabric with sharp scissors; I then finished off the edge with a line of machine satin stitch, supported by a layer of tearaway foundation fabric.

MOA FEATHER

The moa has disappeared into the mists of time – but perhaps a single feather has a tale to tell …?

When the Maori arrived in New Zealand there were no indigenous mammals (apart from one species of bat – see p40), but many types of bird. Presumably the reason that the native birds are so much tamer than their UK relatives is because they have no natural wild predators – no native cats, dogs etc. As a result the bird life is abundant and relatively fearless: we once spent about ten minutes mesmerised by a beautiful crested quail which had moseyed out of the hedge, realised that there were two living things about a thousand times its size nearby, and stood there trying to look nonchalant while it worked out how to beat a dignified retreat. On another occasion a whole family of crested quail performed a cabaret under the trees, their tiny offspring zipping around in random directions like little fluffy wind-up toys.

The birdlife at the subtropical top of the north island is particularly mesmerising. Hyperactive fantails (one's shown in the Kaikura mural above) leap so manically from perch to perch that you long to reach for the Ritalin; tuis call from the trees with their woody cries which make them sound as though they've swallowed miniature sets of panpipes and are trying, ever so genteelly, to cough them back up again. NZ pigeons (bigger, fatter and with more attitude than our versions) bend the small boughs of trees, and NZ kingfishers (bigger, tamer and more numerous than ours) preen themselves alongside. White-throated cormorants roost in the trees (at eye level on some of the bush walks), and, if you're lucky, you'll catch a glimpse of a kakapo, a flightless parrot unique to New Zealand.

One bird you're unlikely to come across is the moa. These enormous flightless birds, which could be up to 10ft (3m) tall and weigh up to 550lb (250kg) were an easy catch and provided a double source of treasure for the early Maori settlers. First of all, of course, they were an excellent source of food; their feathers were also used in the Maori's arts and crafts. By the early 16th century the moa had been hunted to extinction – and yet, as with the Loch Ness Monster, sightings still continue. Perhaps, in the depths of the untamed bush, a family of moa still survive. Maybe they've evolved into a new superspecies; perhaps their plumage has developed from the rather dowdy small brown feathers familiar to the Maori into glorious peacock-like plumes; perhaps shimmering multicoloured giants strut their stuff in some sundrenched glade in the forest, away from prying eyes. A girl can dream, can't she?

Find out more ...

If you'd like to know more about the bird life of the country, try these titles:

Field Guide to the Birds of New Zealand by B Heather and H Robertson, published by Penguin Books New Zealand, ISBN 100143020404 (some sources recommend the more portable and concise *Hand Guide ...* instead).

Kiwi: New Zealand's remarkable bird by N Peat, published by Godwit, ISBN 9781869620462

Also, the Mount Bruce National Wildlife Centre, near the bottom of the south island, has a strong focus on birdlife: www.mtbruce.doc.govt.nz

THE TECHNIQUE

When you want fabric paint colours to blend (as opposed to staying exactly where you put them), silk paint works better than conventional fabric paints as the silk paints are designed to flow freely. After I'd drawn the outline of the feather onto white cotton fabric I sprayed the fabric with water, which helped the colours to flow and prevented tidemarks. I used a large, soft brush to paint on dilute shades of pink, purple and turquoise, then used the same brush to blend the paint on the fabric when the different colours met. The patches of metallic paint were created with glitter mixed into a clear fabric-paint base.

PEBBLES

A quotation spelt out on stones captures the emotion of explorers setting eyes on the new land.

As we travelled the road between Nelson and the Abel Tasman National Park, we were intrigued to see a stretch of sand decorated in an unusual way. On the banks of an estuary, at low tide, it had obviously become a popular pastime to create artworks in the wet sand using pebbles. Alongside the usual D LUVS B etc, there were long messages and also quite sophisticated pictures: sunrises, hearts, flowers, trees etc – several miles of them. Such labours of love – and yet ephemeral, as presumably they're washed away, or at least partly eroded, by the next high tide.

I'm a great fan of land art, and in particular the work of Andy Goldsworthy – and recently I've seen beautiful examples of Nils-Udo's work in a similar vein. I love the idea of taking something from nature – possibly something that's already lovely in its own right, or perhaps something that's quite ordinary – and making a new and beautiful artefact out of it. These examples of simple land art that we saw near Abel Tasman struck echoes with something we'd seen nearer home, at a seaside town in Suffolk where someone had created a house name by painting individual white letters on different-coloured pebbles. I liked the idea of using a quotation from a New Zealand poem, and making a quilt which looked as though I'd written the quotation on pebbles laid in wet sand at low tide.

I wanted a quotation to do with the sea or shore itself, and it took me quite a while to track down just what I was looking for – a passage from a poem by Allen Curnow, a celebrated New Zealand poet, called _Landfall in Unknown_

Seas. This was a perfect choice because it was written to celebrate the 300th anniversary of Abel Tasman's discovery of New Zealand on December 13th 1642 – which tied in nicely with the road up to the Abel Tasman National Park. The quotation I picked captures the moment when, after weeks on open seas, the sailors got their first glimpse of this new, virgin country:

> *'... There was the seascape*
> *Crammed with coast, surprising*
> *As new lands will, the sailor*
> *Moving on the face of the waters ...'*

The words of *Landfall in Unknown Seas* have also been set to music by NZ composer Douglas Lilburn, and the work was broadcast over the radio on the anniversary day itself. Allen Curnow died in 2001, but I contacted his estate and was delighted when they gave me permission to use the quotation on this quilt.

Find out more ...

The quotation from Allen Curnow's poem *Landfall in Unknown Seas* is produced by kind permission of the copyright holder, Mrs Jenifer Curnow. If you'd like to read more of Allen Curnow's poetry, try the collection called *Early Days Yet: New and Collected Poems 1941-1997*, published by Carcanet (ISBN 1 85754 297 5).

The Seafarers Memorial by Grant Palliser, on the seafront in Nelson

---

INSIDE INFORMATION

Materials

Cotton fabrics, net

Quilting

To give the pebble shapes extra dimension I free-quilted round each one randomly (which also appliquéd the shapes to the background). For the sand I used a shaded cotton, and quilted by hand in random lines of big-stitch quilting to suggest the ripples left on the sand by the receding waves.

Backing and binding

Although I did the binding separately, I used the same fabric that I picked for the backing: this pebble print was irresistible.

SHEEP

A study in black and white: a flock of quilted sheep gazes out at a passer-by.

I bet you're impressed that I've got this far in the book and barely mentioned sheep! You remember when people from the UK first started travelling to New Zealand, they would come back with those T-shirts carrying slogans such as 'there are ten million sheep in New Zealand – and I've seen every single one of them!'? Well, it's true: there are a lot of sheep in New Zealand. Not as many as there were, as some sheep farmers are going over to dairy, or to venison, but – especially on the south island – there are still plenty of sheep around. So, they had to be the stars of at least *one* quilt.

You know what it's like when you're out for a walk in the countryside, and you're heading across a field full of sheep. You know the way that sheep always seem to be docile, following each other from field to field, chomping happily: then one of them spots you. Its head turns. And

Sheep sculptures in the centre of Hastings

Sheep in the shade at Te Mata, near Napier

suddenly, as if by ESP, all the others become aware that there's an alien in their midst – and they *all* turn simultaneously and look at you. That's the moment I wanted to capture on this design – that slightly manic, slightly panicky, slightly psychotic look of all those pairs of eyes as they stare at you. What you've got to remember, as one of our friends said, is that there's absolutely nothing going on between those eyes … I made all the head shapes subtly different, to give them slightly varied expressions; after all, although they all look the same to us, I'm sure they're individuals as far as their mothers are concerned.

Find out more …

www.sheepskinstore.co.nz, as you'd expect, sells goods made from the fleeces of the local residents.

Golden Shears (www.goldenshears.co.nz) is a four-day event of sheep-shearing and related activities; it takes place in the Wairarapa district each spring.

www.recipes.co.nz, www.foodworks.co.nz and www. beeflamb.co.nz all have delicious ideas for ways of enjoying one of New Zealand's great ingredients …

MAKE YOUR OWN

If you'd like to create your own version of *Sheep*, you'll find the instructions on page 94.

If you'd like to create your own version of *Sheep*, you'll find the instructions on page 94.

INSIDE INFORMATION

Materials

Cotton fabrics, fabric paint, beads

Quilting

The sheep's bodies and heads are hand-quilted in black cotton thread.

Backing and binding

I used a single piece of verdant green print fabric for the backing and binding, bringing it over the edges of the quilt to create a contrast binding on the front.

Materials

Silk dupion, black cotton fabric

Quilting

To create the effect of domed pots, I only quilted the individual shapes round the edges so that the centres would curve outwards slightly; the quilting (done with lines of black machine stitching) also appliqués the silk to the black cotton and seals the raw edges. On the kawakawa leaves I used the lines of stitching forming the veins of the leaves to appliqué them to the column.

Backing and edging

The backing for the column is a layer of plain black cotton fabric; the random stitching that edges all the shapes has become the quilt's edging too. To seal the layers of the quilt sandwich I cut away the black stitched edge with sharp scissors and then added a line of close zigzag.

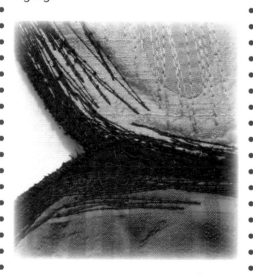

HUNDERTWASSER

The colourful dreams of a surrealist decorate one of the north island's great tourist attractions – a public toilet. (Honest!)

New Zealanders are great patrons of the arts and crafts, both corporately and privately; Wellington in particular seemed full of spectacular sculptures (see pages 55 and 63), and often even tiny towns have art and craft galleries full of items I'd gladly have given a home to. Landscapes, abstracts, local fauna and flora, and Maori designs both traditional and contemporary, all appear in paint, wood, glass, ceramics, metal, textiles.

One of the more unusual public commissions has made the tiny town of Kawakawa (population 1,300) famous. In 1997 the Austrian surrealist Hundertwasser, who had settled on a nearby farm, was asked to design the town's public toilet. Frederick/Friedrich Hundertwasser, born Friedrich Stowasser in Vienna in 1928, was a painter and architect whose unique style in buildings often included bright colours counterpointed against black and white patterns; his own house in Vienna has to be seen to be believed. (If you're familiar with the work of Antoni Gaudi, you'll be thinking along the right lines …) In 1949 he changed his name, and from the early 70s onwards made his home in New Zealand; in 1986 he took out NZ citizenship, and in 1990 was declared a Living Treasure of New Zealand.

Being envisioned by a surrealist, these toilets were never going to be sterile cubicles of white tile, but the final results probably exceeded even the expectations of the commissioning board. The artist included many recycled materials in the design, using coloured glass bottles set in concrete to create windows (clever – it gets over the classic loo problem of allowing in light while obscuring the view in), and crazy paving made from broken tiles covers many

of the surfaces in a mad rigid patchwork, alongside tiles
made by local schoolchildren. A favourite motif in
Hundertwasser's work was the column made from
brightly-coloured ceramic pots and dishes, and columns
in this style create a grand entrance to the toilet block –
which is topped off by a turf roof cheerfully sprouting
seedheads. And up one of these pillars grows a kawakawa
bush with its distinctive heart-shaped leaves; the bush was
planted by a local *kaumatua* (Maori elder) on the day of
Hundertwasser's memorial service.

The toilets have become a massive attraction, but they're
still the town's loos, so as hordes of tourists hover taking
photographs, intrepid locals will thread their way through
with murmured apologies to use the facilities. Hundertwasser died of a heart attack on the QE2 in the year 2000;
he is buried in New Zealand. I must admit it did amuse
me that a public toilet was the final commission of a man
whose adopted name means 'hundred waters' … The bright
column was an irresistible draw when I was planning the
series of quilts; I've made mine in bright silks, to give the
impression of the light catching the ceramics. And from
the bottom creeps up a bright kawakawa plant.

Find out more …

If you'd like to see more of Hundertwasser's work, the book
Hundertwasser: Kunst Haus Wien published by Taschen
(ISBN 3 8 228 6613 X) is a great little introduction; I think
it was the catalogue of a show of the artist's work, and it
has text in German, English and French.

MAKE YOUR OWN

If you'd like to create your own version of
Hundertwasser, you'll find the instructions on
page 95.

AOTEAROA

That first glimpse of The Land of the Long White Cloud ...

The first people to populate New Zealand were the Maori, but no-one knows when they first came to the islands. Some historians believe that Maori may have first arrived around 2,000 years ago, but couldn't sustain life on the islands for long in those early settlements. According to Maori legend the Polynesian explorer Kupe, from Hawaiki, was the first person to discover the islands (dates differ, but sometime between 800-950AD) – he then returned to his native island with reports of the country and how to find it, which were used four centuries later to guide a fleet of canoes to their new homeland.

What does seem certain is that sometime around 12-1300AD the Pacific Islanders became desperately short of space for cultivation and to raise their families, and also beset by intertribal and interisland warfare, and set out on voyages to discover and settle new lands – which included coming to New Zealand. Whenever they arrived, they brought with them rats (including the _kiore_, the Polynesian rat, considered a particular delicacy when fattened on tasty local berries), the _kuri_ or native dog, and their staple food _kumara_ (sweet potato), which grew very well in the new land and enabled the Maori to sustain their settlement of this new country.

The Maori story tells that Kupe's exploring party was drawn to the islands by the sight of a long cloud over the sea: they knew that where there was cloud, there was probably land. Kupe's wife accordingly gave the land the name of Aotearoa, the Land of the Long White Cloud. I like to think of them drawing closer and closer to the cloud, wondering (like Abel Tasman, see page 69) if that was land they could see underneath it or just a mirage. Then, through the clouds, they began to see their first glimpses of a tropical island that looked like their homeland: palm trees reaching down to caramel sands. And so large, compared with their tiny island homes! So much fertile, virgin land just waiting to be mastered. It must have been like rediscovering Eden. This is the moment I've tried to capture in my final quilt, using shadow quilting with an overlay of sheer fabric to represent the cloud, then cutting it away in the shape of the letterforms to reveal the new island paradise.

Find out more ...

Maori: A Photographic and Social History by Michael King, Raupo Publishing (NZ) Ltd (ISBN 9780143010883), gives insight into many different aspects of Maori life.

MAKE YOUR OWN

If you'd like to create your own version of *Aotearoa*, you'll find the instructions on page 96.

If you'd like to create your own version of *Aotearoa*, you'll find the instructions on page 96.

INSIDE INFORMATION

Materials

Cotton print fabrics, synthetic sheer fabric

Quilting

As the whole theme of this quilt is clouds I based most of the quilting design around the cloud-patterned fabric, working free machine quilting around the edges of the clouds and then echoing these lines in the plainer parts of the sky. The letters are padded with an extra layer of wadding to make them stand out more from the surroundings.

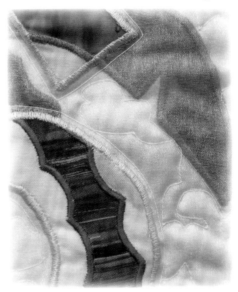

Backing and binding

The back of the quilt is a mottled blue fabric which complements the background of the sky print. A cotton binding didn't look quite right on this quilt, so I picked a white satin binding for the edges which complemented the sheen of the sheer overlay fabric.

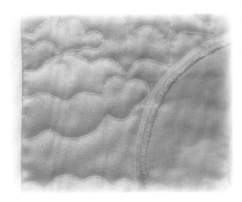

On the following pages I've included patterns and instructions for around half the quilts in the main collection. To help you get the most out of these projects, here are a few basic guidelines.

Hints on ...

... enlarging designs

Where it's necessary to enlarge the quilt design, the best way is to use the grid method. Use a roll of plain paper (wallpaper lining paper works well) so that you don't have to stick sheets together.

1 On the paper draw a grid of 5in (12.5cm) squares, so that there are eight squares down the long side and two across the short side (**a**) and the whole design measures 40 x 10in (1m x 25cm). You'll find that each design in this section has a similar grid of smaller squares over it.

2 Copy the main lines of the design into the squares of your drawn grid, enlarging as you go (**b**); once you're happy with the main lines, fill in any details (**c**). Go over the lines of the design with a black felt pen to make them stronger.

... doing reverse appliqué

Several of the designs in this section use a very simple method of reverse appliqué; this technique cuts your fabric to shape and attaches it to the background all in one go, so that you don't need templates. You'll find curved-tip appliqué scissors very useful for the trimming; use the scissors horizontally, so that the blades slide between the layers of fabric.

1 Press the fabric you're using for the appliqué and lay it right side down on a flat surface. Position the marked fabric, with the drawn side up, on top and pin (**d**).

2 Set your machine to a small zigzag (about 1.5 length and width) and stitch along the lines edging the relevant patch or patches (**e**). On the front of the work, use the small scissors to trim the excess appliqué fabric carefully away from outside the lines of zigzag, taking care not to cut the underneath fabric (**f**).

3 Continue building up the design until all the patches are in place (**g**).

... applying fusible bias binding

You can stitch by hand or machine, using various methods – simply choose the one you like doing best:

- If you're stitching by machine, use a tiny zigzag down each long edge of the binding strips.

- If you're confident with a twin needle, you can stitch both sides at the same time; you'll need a 4mm twin needle and a second reel of cotton to match your bias binding colour. Still use a tiny zigzag (your zigzag foot should still have room for a very small zigzag, even with the twin needle – check this first before you start stitching: hold onto the threads, and move the wheel of your machine forward slowly twice to ensure that both needles clear the needle plate).

- If you're using gold or silver binding for a variation of this design, you can stitch it on using invisible machine appliqué; use a fine monofilament nylon thread in the top of the machine, and a pale cotton thread underneath, and stitch down each side with a very small blind hemming stitch.

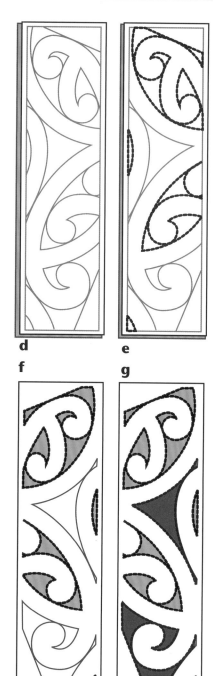

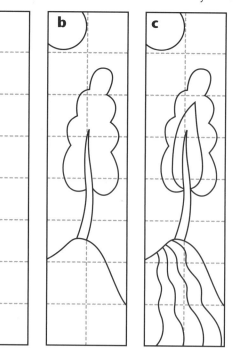

- If you're stitching by hand, use slipstitch or hemstitch – whatever you'd usually use for hand appliqué.

... binding your quilts

I find it most satisfactory to bind my quilts with a continuous strip, rather than binding each edge individually. Unless the quilt has a curved edge or corners, you can use a binding strip cut on the straight grain.

... hanging methods

Quilts this small are easy to hang.

- You can add a hidden casing on the back. Cut a 10 x 3in (25 x 8cm) rectangle of fabric, then turn in and press a small double hem all the way around; machine stitch. Slipstitch the casing to the back of the quilt at the top, then slip through a plain or fancy hanging rod or batten.

- You can add hanging loops of fabric, ribbon or tape to the top edge then slip them over a pretty quilt-hanging rod.

- With a piece this size you can stitch a curtain ring to each top corner of the quilt back, then hang the rings on a couple of hooks on the wall.

Seascape PATTERN

YOU WILL NEED:

- 40 x 10in (1m x 25cm) white cotton foundation fabric
- 40 x 10in (1m x 25cm) piece of flat wadding
- 40 x 10in (1m x 25cm) piece of backing fabric
- quilting threads for your choice of hand or machine quilting
- 3yd (3m) strip of fabric for binding (I used a strip of silk 1½in/4cm wide)
- 12in (30cm)-long strips of assorted cotton, silk and sheer fabrics, in sand and sea colours, varying from light to dark

- rotary cutter, ruler and board
- pencil
- beads, shell fragments etc (optional)

INSTRUCTIONS

1 Across the foundation fabric draw straight lines at random intervals and angles to create a basic background for your seascape (**a**). The lowest 3 or 4 strips will be sand/shoreline, and the others will create the sea.

2 Decide which fabric to use where, grading from sand at the bottom of the design, through pale sea colours, to dark at the top. Pin or tape a small snippet of each fabric to the relevant patch to remind you which fabric goes where. Pin the lowest piece of fabric onto the front (unmarked) side of the foundation fabric, so that it comfortably covers the first segment of the design (**b**).

3 Pin the second fabric strip on top of the first, right sides together; on

the back (marked side) of the work, stitch by machine along the first marked line (**c**). Trim the raw edges of the patches to ¼in beyond the seam line, and press the second patch open (**d**).

4 Continue adding patches in the same way until all your patches are in position (**e**). Layer the design with the wadding and backing fabric, then add layers of sheer fabric on the front of the work to add depth (**f**), securing them with random lines of machine stitching.

5 Add more lines of quilting by hand or machine; if you want to couch down fine cord for texture, you can either catch it with a small machine zigzag or wind it onto the bobbin and stitch from the back of the work. Once you feel you have done enough quilting, trim the edges of the work neatly with the rotary cutter, and bind the outside edges as you wish.

6 Add any extra embellishments such as beads, charms, shells etc.

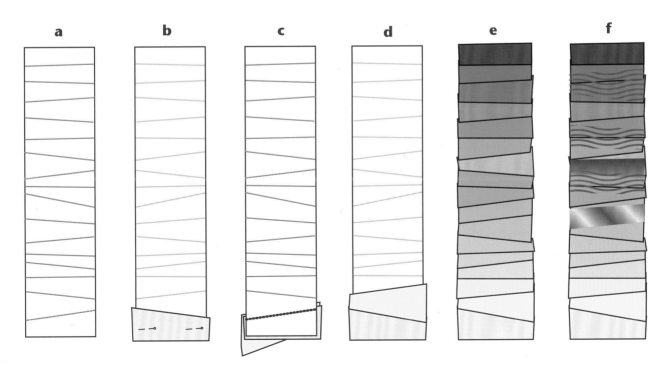

a   b   c   d   e   f

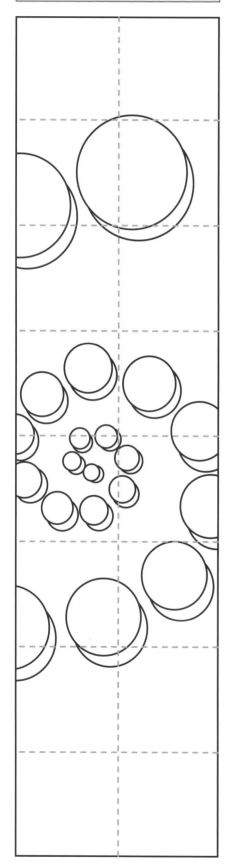

Stone Spiral PATTERN

YOU WILL NEED:

- 40 x 10in (1m x 25cm) brown batik background fabric
- 40 x 10in (1m x 25cm) piece of flat wadding
- 40 x 10in (1m x 25cm) piece of backing fabric
- quilting threads for your choice of hand or machine quilting
- assorted 'stone-print' fabrics, eg brown and beige batiks and marbled cottons
- large scrap of dark brown print or plain fabric for the shadows
- 3yd (3m) strip of fabric for binding (I used a strip 1½in/4cm wide)
- 20 x 10in (50 x 25cm) double-sided bonding web
- pencil, ruler
- plain paper for enlarging the design, and a black felt pen
- scraps of extra wadding for padding the stone shapes (optional)

INSTRUCTIONS

1   Enlarge the quilt design as described on page 76. On the paper side of the bonding web, trace all the circles and part-circles, plus their shadows (**a**) – mark the number on each circle and its corresponding shadow, just so that you don't get them mixed up.

2   Cut the shapes out roughly, outside the marked lines. Choose which fabric you want to use for which stone, then fuse the relevant circle onto the back of each fabric; cut all the shapes out along the marked lines (**b**). (If you'd like to add extra padding to your stones, cut a matching shape in wadding for each one at this stage.) Fuse all the shadow sections of bonding web onto the back of the shadow fabric, and cut out the shapes along the marked lines.

3   Press the background fabric and lay it right side up on a flat surface. Peel the paper backings off the stone circles and arrange them in a pleasing spiral (**c**), using the full-size pattern as a rough guide for positioning them (remember that the pattern is the other way around from your finished design).

4   One you're happy with the positions of the stones, peel the papers off the shadow sections one at a time, slip each one under its matching stone, then fuse that stone and shadow in place. Continue until all the stones and shadows are in position (**d**).

5   If you're adding extra wadding circles, pin them behind the matching stones now. Layer the quilt top with the wadding and backing fabric, and quilt as you wish by hand or machine; finish off the quilt by binding the outside edges.

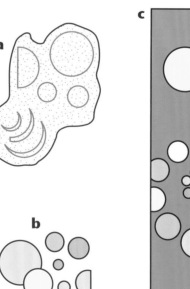

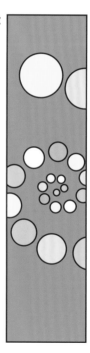

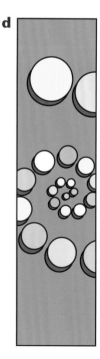

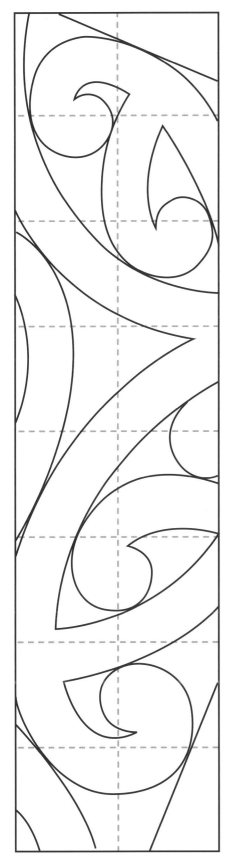

Maori Curves
PATTERN

YOU WILL NEED:

- 40 x 10in (1m x 25cm) white print cotton fabric
- 40 x 10in (1m x 25cm) red print cotton fabric
- 40 x 10in (1m x 25cm) black print cotton fabric
- 40 x 10in (1m x 25cm) piece of flat wadding
- 40 x 10in (1m x 25cm) piece of backing fabric
- quilting threads for your choice of hand or machine quilting
- 7½yd (7m) black fusible bias binding, ¼in (6mm) wide
- 3yd (3m) strip of fabric for binding (I used a strip 1¼in/3.5cm wide)
- black thread for appliqué and adding the bias binding
- soft pencil, ruler
- plain paper for enlarging the design, and a black felt pen
- small, sharp-pointed scissors

INSTRUCTIONS

1 Enlarge the quilt design as described on page 76. Press the white fabric and lay it, right side down, over the design; pin the layers together, then use pencil to trace all the lines of the design (**a**).

2 Follow the instructions for reverse appliqué on page 76 to add first of all the red fabric patches and then the black ones (**b**). Press the design and position it on top of the wadding (don't add the backing at this stage).

3 Cover all the lines of stitching with fusible binding, pressing it firmly into place and folding it sharply at any corners (**c**), then stitch the binding on (on page 76 you'll find various different methods you can use for attaching the fusible binding).

4 Add the backing fabric to the layers of your quilt and add any extra hand or machine quilting you fancy; finish off the quilt by binding the outside edges.

a  **b**  **c**

Pukeko PATTERN

YOU WILL NEED:

- 40 x 10in (1m x 25cm) piece of felt for the backing
- 26 x 10in (70 x 25cm) piece of pale blue felt for the sky
- 6 x 10in (15 x 25cm) piece of pale turquoise or aqua felt for the river
- 10in (25cm) square of yellow felt for the ground
- 10in (25cm) square of mid turquoise or aqua felt for the pond
- 2in-wide (5cm-wide) strips of felt for the borders; the longest four strips need to be 22in (56cm) long
- large scraps of felt in other colours for the other parts of the design
- quilting threads for your choice of hand or machine quilting
- pencil, ruler
- plain paper for enlarging the design
- greaseproof or tracing paper
- small beads or buttons for decoration (optional), and for the pukeko's eye
- cord for the bulrush stems (optional)

INSTRUCTIONS

1 Enlarge the quilt design as described on page 76. On the greaseproof/tracing paper, trace all the patches individually (including the dotted lines, which mark where some shapes go under others); mark all the shapes with their names, and cut them out.

2 Use these paper templates to cut the individual patches from the felt; leave the papers pinned loosely to the shapes so that you can remember which bit goes where (**a**)!

3 Lay the background piece of felt on a flat surface and position the sky patch at the top, matching the raw edges, and the pond patch at the bottom. Now lay the river patch at the bottom of the sky so that it covers the raw edge, and position the ground piece on top so that it covers the raw edges of the river and the pond (**b**). Pin these patches in place, and work decorative stitches along the top of the river and the edges of the ground to secure them. (Throughout this project it doesn't matter if your patches aren't in exactly the same position as mine, as long as your design works well.)

4 Pin in position the bulrush leaves, and the waterlilies and their leaves; secure these patches with decorative stitching (**c**). If you like you can also add smaller felt shapes on top of the leaves to decorate them. Now add the heads of the bulrushes (plus extra decoration if you want), and stitch the stems using machine stitching or couched cord (**d**).

5 Use the same method to add the pukeko and the rocks (**e**). (At this stage I also added a decorative butterfly and dragonfly to keep my pukeko company.) Finally, add the side borders and their central details, and the top and bottom borders (**f**). Add the pukeko's eye, and embellish the rest of the design with little beads or buttons if you wish.

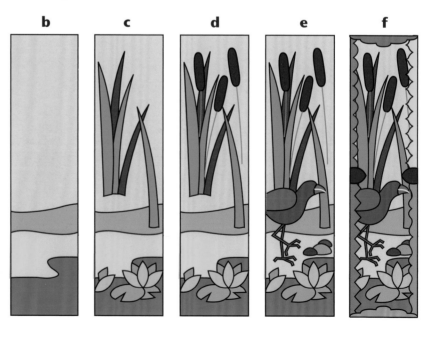

b   **c**   **d**   **e**   **f**

Pohutukawa PATTERN

YOU WILL NEED:

- 40 x 10in (1m x 25cm) cream/gold print background fabric
- 40 x 10in (1m x 25cm) piece of flat wadding
- 40 x 10in (1m x 25cm) piece of backing fabric
- quilting threads for your choice of hand or machine quilting
- 16 circles of assorted red sheer fabrics, each one roughly 14in (36cm) in diameter
- dark green and mid green cotton fabrics for the leaves, four 12 x 2in (30 x 5cm) strips of each (or two 24 x 2in/60 x 5cm strips of each)
- large scraps of the dark green fabric for the bases of the flowers
- green or invisible thread for stitching on the appliqué shapes
- 3yd (3m) strip of fabric for binding (I used a strip 2in/5cm wide)
- double-sided bonding web, one piece 5 x 10in (13 x 25cm), and four 12 x 3in (30 x 8cm) strips (or two 24 x 3in/60 x 8cm strips)
- pencil
- small yellow beads (optional)

INSTRUCTIONS

1 Join each strip of dark green fabric to a light strip, and press the seams open. On the paper side of the bonding web, trace eight leaf shapes onto the strips and four calyx shapes onto the extra piece (trace some calyxes the other way around for variety); cut the shapes out roughly, outside the drawn lines (**a**). Fuse the leaf shapes onto the wrong side of the joined fabric strips, aligning the points with the seam, and cut out (**b**); fuse the calyx shapes onto the wrong side of the remaining green fabric and cut out (**c**).

2 Pile the sheer red fabric circles on top of each other and use large scissors to cut random shapes out of the edges to make them less even (**d**).

Now divide the circles into four sets of four, mixing up the different fabrics, and fold each set into quarters (**e**); don't try to keep the edges of the circles even.

3 Press the background fabric and lay it right side up; peel the paper backings off the leaves and calyxes and arrange them in an attractive design (I only used seven leaves). Once you're happy with the layout, pin a cone of red sheers behind each calyx (**f**); each red cone should conceal the end of the stem above it. Fuse all the green fabric shapes into place – make sure that the iron doesn't touch the sheer fabrics, just in case they melt.

4 Layer the quilt top with the wadding and backing fabric. Attach the green shapes by machine-stitching round the edges, then secure the red shapes with random lines of hand or machine quilting. Add any other hand or machine quilting that you wish, then finish off the quilt by binding the outside edges. If you're using beads, stitch these onto the tops of the blossoms in a random design.

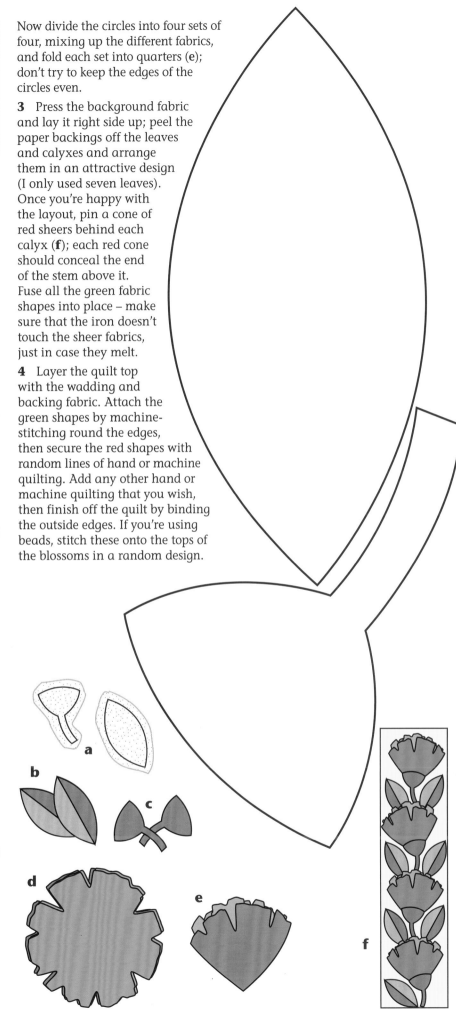

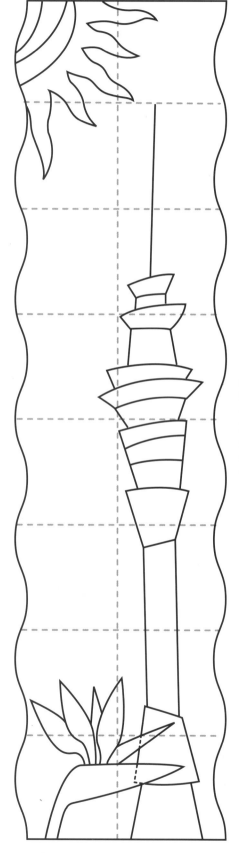

Sky Tower PATTERN

YOU WILL NEED:

- 40 x 10in (1m x 25cm) cheerful background fabric (I used yellow)
- 40 x 10in (1m x 25cm) piece of flat wadding
- 40 x 10in (1m x 25cm) piece of backing fabric
- quilting threads for your choice of hand or machine quilting
- 3yd (3m) bias binding (I used multicoloured satin binding, 1in/2.5cm wide finished size)
- machine-stitching threads in bright colours
- plain paper for enlarging the design, and a black felt pen
- pencil, ruler and tracing (or greaseproof) paper
- patches of cotton fabrics in bright prints and plains for the Sky Tower, the sun and the flower
- beads and buttons in bright colours for decoration
- 40 x 10in (1m x 25cm) piece of Stitch 'n' Tear or other tearaway foundation paper
- bobbin fill for the zigzag (optional)

INSTRUCTIONS

1 Enlarge the quilt design as described on page 76. Lay the background fabric right side up over the full-size drawing and trace the lines in pencil (**a**). If you'd like to make the edges of the finished quilt wavy, trace the curved outside edge too at this stage.

2 Trace the different shapes of the design individually onto tracing or greaseproof paper. Use these paper templates to cut the fabric patches, always positioning the template right side up on the right side of the fabric. Cut the patches fractionally bigger than the templates all round (**b**) – you're not actually adding a seam allowance, but a scant millimetre will allow you to overlap the patches slightly at step 3. (Tracing the patches allows you to do the design again if you wish.)

3 Pin the patches in position on the background fabric, overlapping them slightly so that there are no gaps; begin with the Sky Tower and zigzag the patches in place round the edges, then add the flower and sun (**c**).

4 Pin the piece of tearaway foundation paper underneath the design, and work a line of machine satin stitch (see p7) to create the spire at the top of the tower. Then work lines of contrasting satin stitch round the coloured patches, beginning with the shapes of the Sky Tower itself then working round the patches of the flower and the sun. Once all the satin stitch is complete, tear away the foundation paper from the back of the design.

5 Layer the quilt top with the wadding and backing, then quilt as you wish by hand or machine. If you're going for the wavy outside edge, trim the layers along the pencil line. Bind the edges to complete the quilt, and embellish as you wish (**d**).

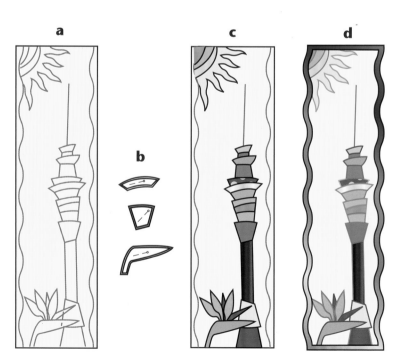

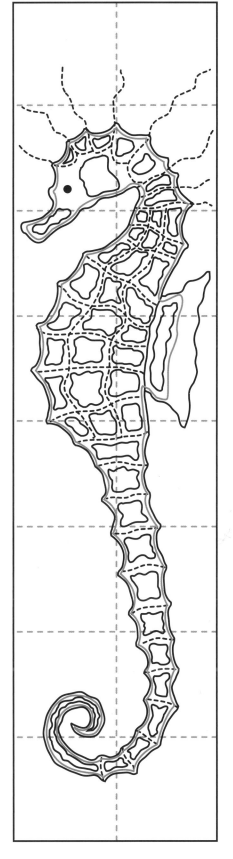

Seahorse PATTERN

YOU WILL NEED:

- 40 x 10in (1m x 25cm) 'sea'-type background fabric
- 40 x 10in (1m x 25cm) piece of flat wadding
- 40 x 10in (1m x 25cm) piece of backing fabric
- quilting threads for your choice of hand or machine quilting
- 3yd (3m) binding
- cotton fabric for the body and contrast fabric for the details, 34 x 10in (90 x 25cm) of each
- double-sided bonding web, 34 x 10in (90 x 25cm)
- machine-stitching thread in a contrasting colour
- thick coton perlé or fine cord in a matching colour (optional)
- plain paper for enlarging the design, black felt pen, pencil, ruler, greaseproof or tracing paper
- single bead for the eye, and extra beads for decoration (optional)
- 40 x 10in (1m x 25cm) piece of Stitch 'n' Tear or other tearaway foundation paper
- small, sharp-pointed scissors or appliqué scissors

INSTRUCTIONS

1 Enlarge the quilt design as described on page 76. Lay the bonding web paper side up over the pattern, and trace all the solid black lines of the design in pencil (**a**); cut the shape out roughly, outside the drawn outline.

2 Press the fabric you're using for the main body of the seahorse, and fuse the bonding web shape onto the back. Use small scissors to cut away all the patches inside the drawn lines and around the edge (**b**).

3 Trace the purple line onto greaseproof or tracing paper, then turn it over and use it to cut a patch from the right side of the contrast fabric. Remove the paper backing from the seahorse shape and pin it, right side up, on the contrast patch so that its raw edges are covered (**c**).

4 Position the seahorse on the background fabric; remove the pins, and fuse the shape into position, trapping the contrast fabric.

5 Sandwich the quilt top with the wadding and the backing, and quilt the background as you wish. Position the tearaway foundation fabric behind the backing. Use a small satin stitch (see p7) to stitch slightly wavy lines over the seahorse's body, roughly as shown by the dotted lines (**d**).

6 Use the same method to create the fronds around the seahorse's head, and the main outlines of the shape (**e**). (I used cord under these final lines for extra dimension.)

7 Remove the tearaway foundation paper and free quilt round the eye. Stitch a bead on in the centre of the eye, and add any other beads you wish to on the body.

8 If you like, add some sea anemones or other sealife shapes around the seahorse. Cut the edges of the quilt into random waves, then bind the edges to complete the quilt.

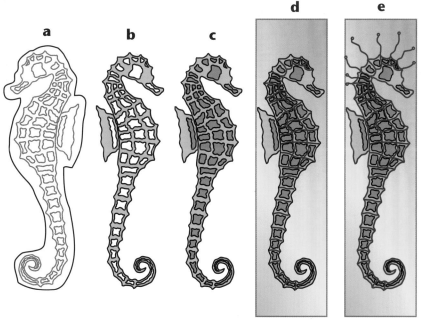

a   b   c   d   e

Flora PATTERN

YOU WILL NEED:

- four 12in (30cm) squares of white cotton, prepared for sunprinting (remember that these have to be kept in the dark till you're ready to print)
- four 12in (30cm) squares of freezer paper
- 40 x 10in (1m x 25cm) piece of flat wadding
- 40 x 10in (1m x 25cm) piece of backing fabric
- quilting threads for your choice of hand or machine quilting
- 3yd (3m) strip of fabric for binding (I used a strip 1¾in/4.5cm wide)
- white or pale blue thread for piecing
- pencil, ruler
- quilt rule, rotary cutter and board
- small, sharp-pointed scissors

INSTRUCTIONS

1 Fold each square of freezer paper exactly into four. Unfold, then position one quarter of the paper over one of the plant motifs, paper (non-shiny) side up, matching the centre points and fold lines. Trace the lines of the design onto the paper.

2 Fold the paper up again (**a**), then carefully cut out the shape with small scissors, making sure that you hold the layers of paper together closely as you cut (**b**). Do the same with the other three designs. If you want to use the 'negatives' of two of the designs (**c**), make sure that you don't cut into these outside bits of paper. If you have little curved-tipped appliqué scissors, you might find them quite useful for cutting out the plant shapes.

3 When you're ready to print (you might have to wait for a good sunny day!), take the squares of prepared fabric out of their lightproof bag and quickly press the freezer paper shapes onto them, shiny side down, centring the paper shapes on the fabric squares. Follow the manufacturer's instructions to 'cure' the fabrics in the sun, then for rinsing and drying (**d**).

4 Trim the squares down to 11in (28cm), making sure that the design is centred in each one, then join with ½in (12mm) seams to create the quilt top (**e**); press the seams to the darker sides. Layer the quilt top with the wadding and backing, then quilt as you wish by hand or machine; trim the quilt to 10in (25cm) wide and bind.

b 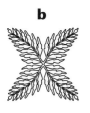 **c**

d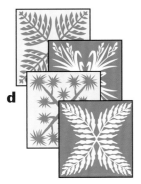

e

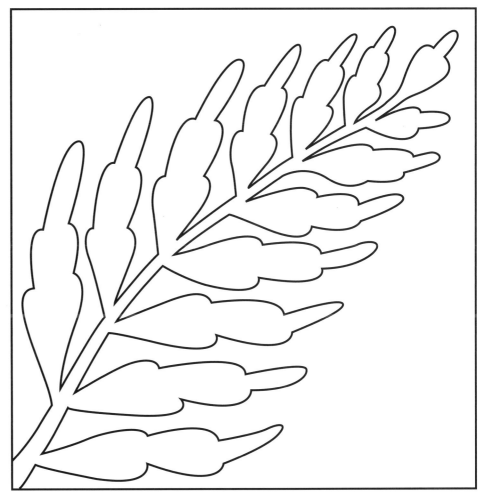

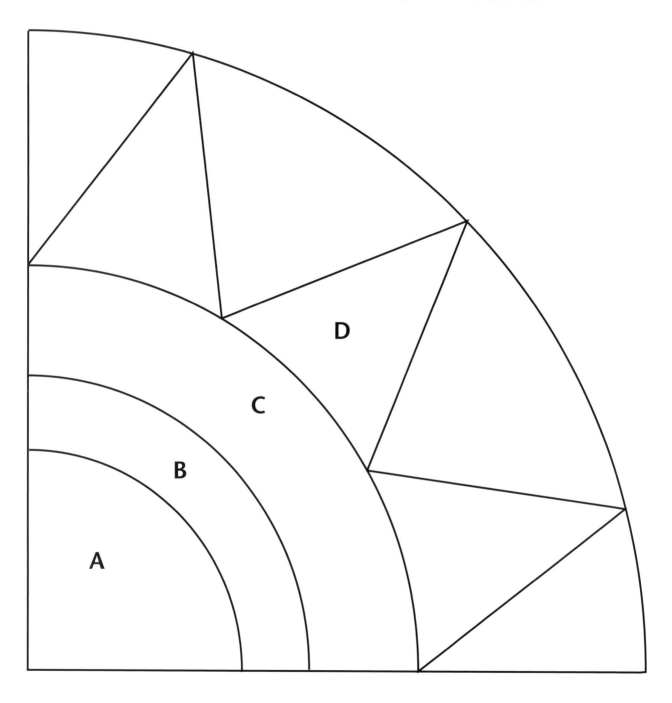

Napier Beauty
PATTERN

YOU WILL NEED:

- four 11in (28cm) background squares of ivory silk
- 40 x 10in (1m x 25cm) piece of silk dupion for the backing
- 40 x 10in (1m x 25cm) piece of flat wadding
- large scraps of silk dupion in mid-pastel colours
- quilting threads for your choice of hand or machine quilting
- 3yd (3m) strip of binding
- pencil, ruler
- freezer paper

INSTRUCTIONS

1 Use a photocopier to enlarge the template by 141% (A4 to A3). Trace all the curved shapes (A, B, C and D) four times each onto the paper side of the freezer paper (**a**) and cut out all the shapes.

2 Choose your colours for each block and foundation-piece the fabrics onto the D arcs as shown (**b**); leave a ¼in (6mm) seam allowance around the edges of the shape.

3 Press the freezer paper shapes onto the backs of your chosen fabrics for the different arcs, shiny side down, and cut out all the shapes leaving a ¼in (6mm) allowance all round (**c**). On the outside edges of each arc (including the foundation-pieced arcs), press the seam allowance under (to the dull side of the freezer paper) as shown (**d**). You may have done this technique with spray starch; I found that the silk dupion didn't require starch.

4 Lay each background square on a flat surface and position the pieces A, B and C and D on top of each other to create each block (**e**). Use invisible machine appliqué around the curves to appliqué all the shapes to each other.

5 Remove all the freezer paper shapes from the back of the work (you will find it useful to trim away the excess ivory silk behind the appliqué shapes), then join the blocks into one long quilt top using ½in (12mm) seams (**f**). Trim the quilt to 10in (25cm) width, layer with the backing fabric and wadding, and quilt as you wish by hand or machine. Bind the raw edges of the quilt to complete it.

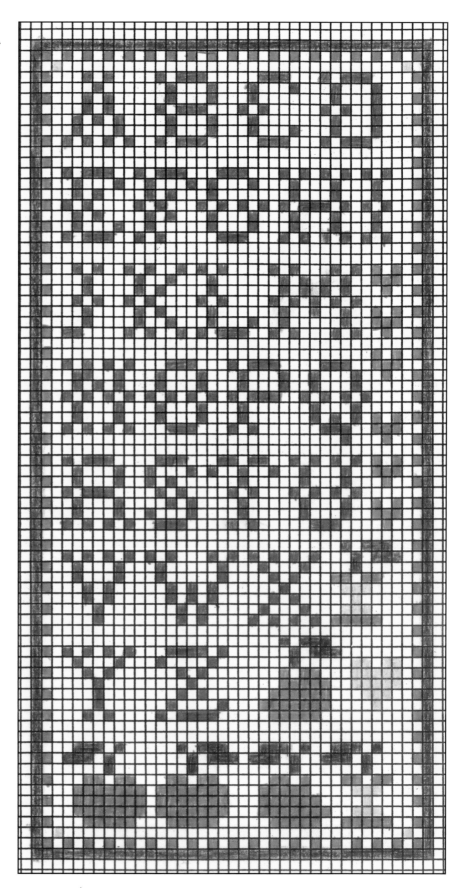

A is for Apple ALPHABET

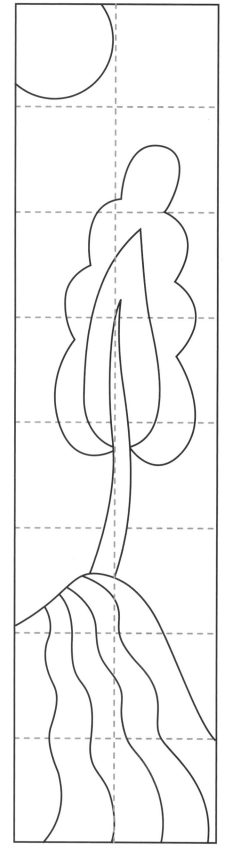

YOU WILL NEED:

- 40 x 10in (1m x 25cm) navy blue cotton background fabric
- 40 x 10in (1m x 25cm) piece of flat wadding
- 40 x 10in (1m x 25cm) piece of backing fabric
- quilting threads for your choice of hand or machine quilting
- 3yd (3m) binding (I used a golden cotton print, 1½ in/4cm wide)
- patches of cotton fabrics in cream, yellow and blue plains and prints; as a guide the main tree piece needs to be 18 x 9in (45 x 23cm), and the largest hill section is 15 x 4in (38 x 10cm)
- machine-stitching threads in yellows and blues
- plain paper for enlarging the design, and a black felt pen
- pencil, ruler, and pale crayon
- beads and fabric paint for decoration (optional)
- 40 x 10in (1m x 25cm) piece of Stitch 'n' Tear or other tearaway foundation paper
- bobbin fill for the zigzag (optional)
- small, sharp-pointed scissors or appliqué scissors

INSTRUCTIONS

1 Enlarge the quilt design as described on page 76. Lay the background fabric wrong side up over the full-size drawing, using a lightbox so that you can see the lines, and trace the lines in pale crayon (**a**). If you don't have a lightbox, pin the background fabric wrong side up over the drawing and tape it to a large window on a sunny day.

2 Press the fabric you're using for the main part of the tree, and pin it right side up on the front of the fabric so that it comfortably covers the area of the tree (hold it up to the light to check once you've pinned it in position). Use the reverse appliqué technique described on page 76 to add the fabric on the main part of the tree (**b**), then use the same technique to add all the other patches (**c**).

3 If you're adding any fabric paint shadows or highlights, now's the time to do it; follow the manufacturer's instructions for using and fixing your particular fabric paint or crayons. Press the design and layer it with the wadding and backing. If you'd like to quilt the background with wavy lines of machine stitching, as I have, do that now.

4 Pin the piece of tearaway foundation paper underneath the design, and work lines of machine satin stitch (see p7) around all the zigzagged edges of the patches; stitch all the lines of the tree and between the hill patches before you work the stitching around the top of the hill.

5 Once all the quilting is complete, remove the tearaway foundation paper. Trim the corners at 45°. Bind the edges to complete the quilt, and embellish with beads (and a kiwi …) if you wish.

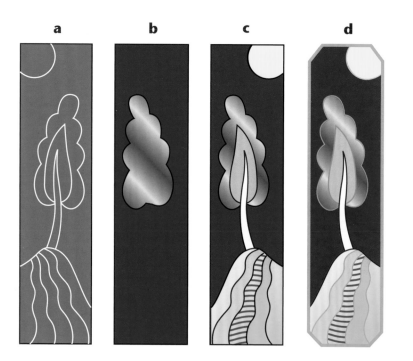

a   b   c   d

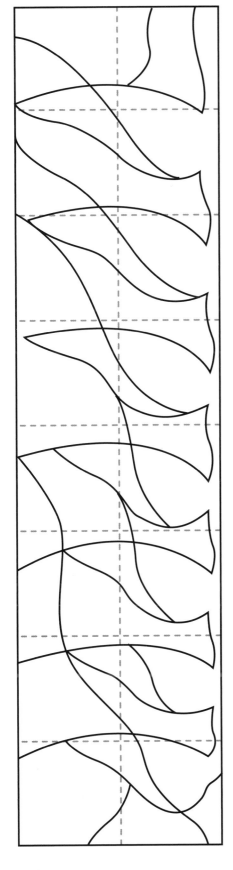

YOU WILL NEED:

- 40 x 10in (1m x 25cm) pale green cotton background fabric (I used a green with a subtle leaf print, which was a good foil for the other green prints and plain fabrics)
- 40 x 10in (1m x 25cm) piece of flat wadding
- 40 x 10in (1m x 25cm) piece of backing fabric
- 40 x 7in (1m x 18cm) piece of red plain or print fabric
- large scraps of different green prints and plains for the background
- large scraps of two or three different yellow print fabrics for the claws
- quilting threads for your choice of hand or machine quilting
- 6½yd (6m) black fusible bias binding, ¼in (6mm) wide
- 3yd (3m) strip of fabric for binding (I used a strip 1¼in/3.5cm wide)
- black thread for appliqué and adding the bias binding
- soft pencil, ruler
- plain paper for enlarging the design, and a black felt pen
- small, sharp-pointed scissors

INSTRUCTIONS

1 Enlarge the quilt design as described on page 76. Press the pale green background fabric and lay it, right side down, over the design; pin the layers together, then use pencil to trace all the lines of the design (**a**).

2 Decide which background patches you'd like to enhance with different green fabrics, and follow the instructions for reverse appliqué on page 76 to add these (**b**). Use the same technique to add the red patch for the main section of the flower, and the yellow patches on the 'claws' (**c**).

3 Press the design and position it on top of the wadding (don't add the backing at this stage). Fuse and stitch the lines marked as thick black lines (**d**); on page 76 you'll find various different methods you can use for attaching the fusible binding. Then add the remaining lines of binding as shown (**e**); begin with the lowest line, fusing and stitching this first, then add the next line up and so on until the design is complete.

4 Add the backing fabric to the layers of your quilt and add any extra hand or machine quilting you fancy; finish off the quilt by binding the outside edges.

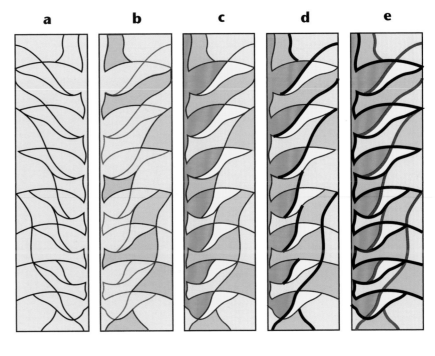

a   b   c   d   e

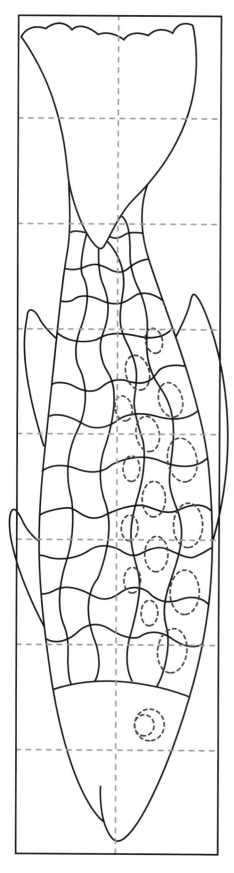

YOU WILL NEED:

- two 28 x 10in (72 x 25cm) pieces of shaded cotton fabric for the main body
- large scraps of cotton fabrics for the head, tail and fins, and small scraps for the spots and the eye
- 40 x 12in (1m x 30cm) piece of flat wadding
- 40 x 12in (1m x 30cm) piece of backing fabric
- quilting threads for your choice of hand or machine quilting
- machine-stitching threads for outlining the main patches
- plain paper, pencil and ruler for enlarging the design
- double-sided bonding web, at least 40 x 18in (1m x 45cm)
- 40 x 12in (1m x 30cm) piece of Stitch 'n' Tear or other tearaway foundation paper
- non-stick ironing sheet

INSTRUCTIONS

1 Enlarge the quilt design as described on page 76. On the paper side of the bonding web, trace the body section twice, and all the other pieces once; draw the horizontal wiggly lines on one body piece, and the vertical ones on the other. Cut all the drawn shapes out roughly, outside the pencil lines (**a**).

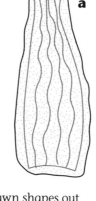

2 Fuse the two body sections onto the wrong sides of the shaded fabrics, then cut out them along the marked edge and cut along the wiggly lines (**b**); number all the cut sections so you don't forget which one is which!

3 Beginning at the head end, weave the cut strips into the shape of the fish's body (**c**). Lay this body shape on the middle of the wadding and press to fuse the woven section, protecting the rest of the wadding with the non-stick sheet.

4 Fuse the bonding web shapes for the head, fins and tail onto the wrong sides of the relevant fabrics, then cut them out and fuse them in position (**d**) – overlap the sections slightly so that there aren't any gaps.

5 Layer the design with the backing fabric and quilt all the different sections as you wish. Fuse the bonding web patches for the spots and the eye onto your chosen fabrics and cut out; fuse the spots onto the fish's body in a pleasing design, and fuse the eye pieces in position on the head (**e**). Go over the shapes with circuits of free machining to attach and decorate them.

6 Once all the quilting is complete, go round the outline of the entire shape with a small zigzag stitch, then trim the excess wadding away. Position the tearaway foundation paper under the quilt and work lines of machine satin stitch (see page 7) around all the edges of the main patches (**f**); remove the paper.

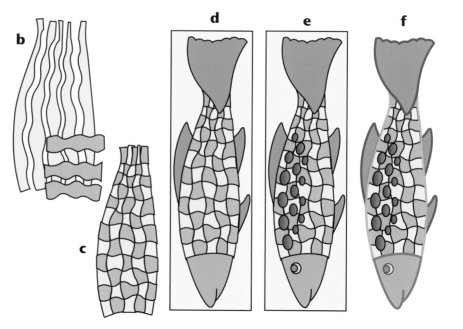

Deco Fern PATTERN

YOU WILL NEED:

- 40 x 10in (1m x 25cm) decorative background fabric in a pale colour; this fabric will show on the front of the work around the ferns, so choose something pretty (I used a cream brocade fabric)
- 40 x 10in (1m x 25cm) piece of flat wadding
- 42 x 12in (107 x 30cm) piece of backing fabric
- large scraps of many different silk dupions or cotton fabrics in your chosen colourscheme (as a guide, the piece for the largest fern needs to be 25 x 10in/65 x 25cm).
- 3yd (3m) strip of fabric for binding the quilt
- quilting threads for your choice of hand or machine quilting
- 6½yd (6m) gold fusible bias binding, ¼in (6mm) wide
- cream thread for the appliqué and for adding the bias binding
- soft pencil, ruler
- plain paper for enlarging the design, and a black felt pen
- small, sharp-pointed scissors
- beads (optional)

INSTRUCTIONS

1 Enlarge the quilt design as described on page 76. Press the pale background fabric and lay it, right side down, over the design; pin the layers together, then use pencil to trace all the lines of the design (**a**).

2 Follow the instructions for reverse appliqué on page 76 to add the patches for the main ferns (**b**), then use the same technique to add the other patches of the design (**c**).

3 Press the design and position it on top of the wadding (don't add the backing at this stage). Fuse and stitch the lines marked as thick black lines (**d**); on page 76 you'll find various different methods you can use for attaching the fusible binding. Use the same technique to add the final series of binding lines as shown (**e**); begin by stitching the top fern, then once you've stitched that, fuse and stitch the next fern and so on, working down to the bottom curve.

4 Add the backing fabric to the layers of your quilt and add any extra hand or machine quilting you fancy; finish off the quilt by binding the outside edges, and embellish with beads if you wish.

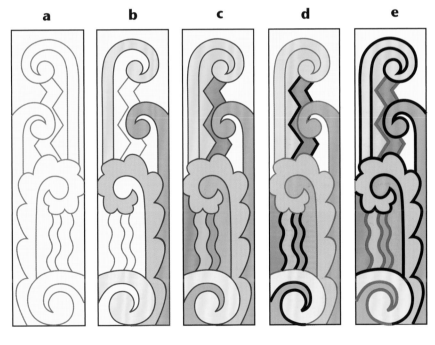

a   b   c   d   e

Bush Fern
PATTERN

YOU WILL NEED:

- 40 x 10in (1m x 25cm) piece of flat wadding
- 40 x 10in (1m x 25cm) piece of backing fabric

- assorted dark green batik fabrics, cut into 1½in/4cm strips
- four 3in (7.5cm) extra squares of batik fabric for the block centres
- quilting threads for your choice of hand or machine quilting
- 3yd (3m) binding (I used another green batik, 1½in/4cm wide)
- four 11in (28cm) squares of Stitch 'n' Tear (or similar)
- pencil, ruler, and pale chalk marker
- green embroidery thread (I used a variegated fine coton perlé)
- rotary cutter, board and quilt rule

INSTRUCTIONS

1 Use a photocopier to enlarge the Log Cabin template by 141% (A4 to A3). Trace the design onto each square of Stitch 'n' Tear; do the tracing in pencil, and use a ruler to keep the lines nice and straight.

2 On the front (unmarked side) of one template, pin a fabric square right side up so that it covers the central patch, then pin a strip of one of the other batiks, right sides facing, so that the raw edges align along the edges of strip 1 (**a**). On the wrong (marked) side of the work, stitch a

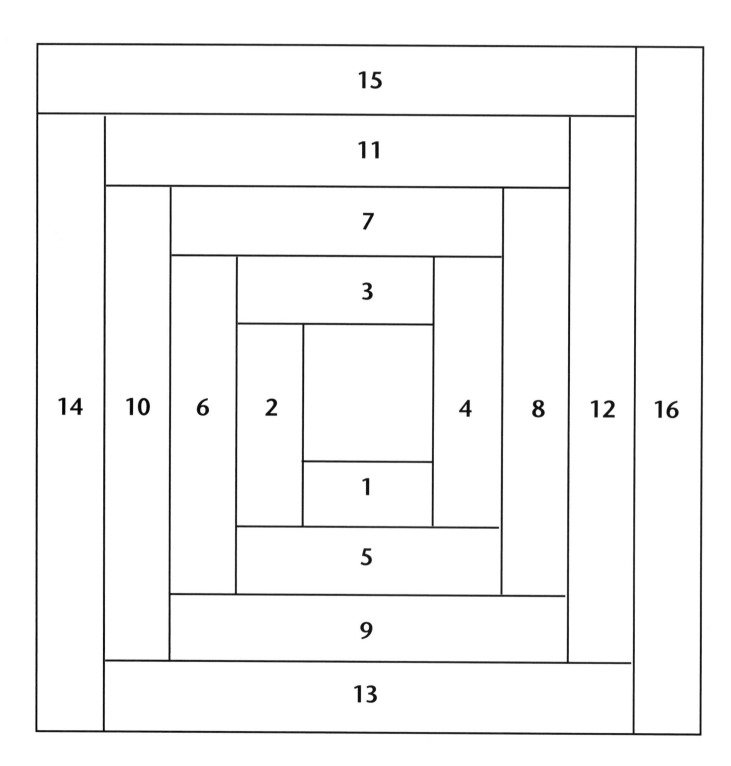

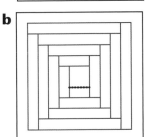

a

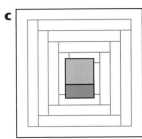

b

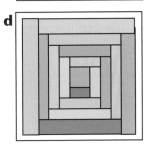

c

d

e

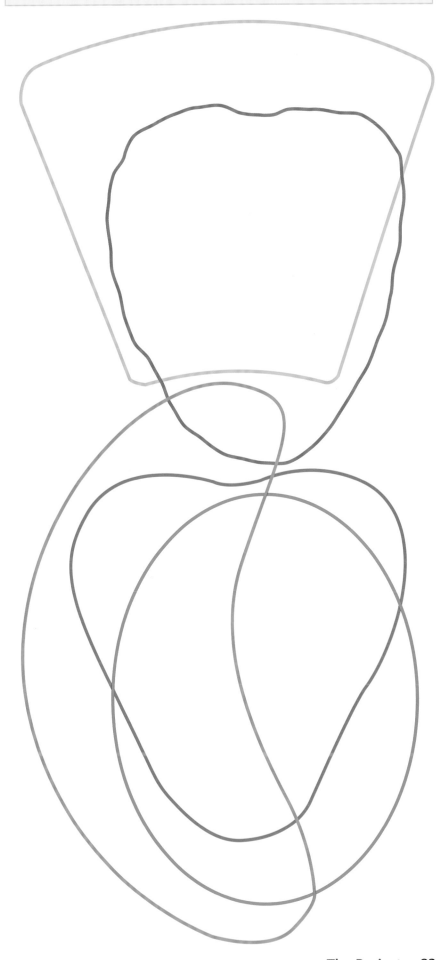

line of straight machining along this edge (**b**). Trim the strip to length, and press open (**c**).

3 Use the same method to add all the strips in turn (**d**); create four Log Cabin blocks in this way. Using the rotary cutter, trim each block (including the Stitch 'n' Tear) to ¼in outside the final drawn line.

4 Join the four blocks to create the quilt top, then use chalk marker to draw a freehand fern shape on the right side (**e**). Layer up the quilt top with the backing and wadding, then use a hand embroidery stitch or a decorative machine stitch to quilt the fern shape. Bind the edges to complete the quilt.

Sheep PATTERN

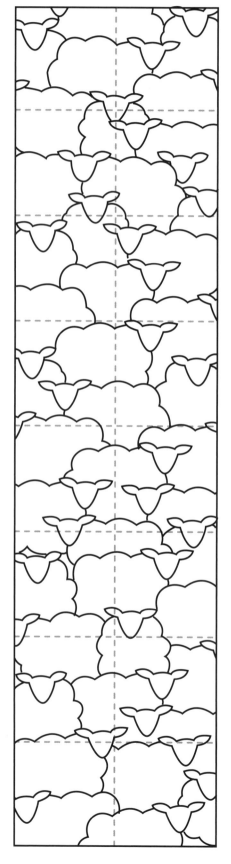

YOU WILL NEED:

- 40 x 10in (1m x 25cm) white cotton background fabric
- 40 x 10in (1m x 25cm) piece of flat wadding
- 42 x 12in (105 x 30cm) piece of backing fabric
- quilting threads for your choice of hand or machine quilting
- plain paper for enlarging the design, and a black felt pen
- grey pencil, ruler
- black fabric paint (the permanent markers made specially for fabric work well)
- pack of small round white beads for the eyes

INSTRUCTIONS

1   Enlarge the quilt design as described on page 76. Lay the background fabric right side up over the full-size drawing and trace the lines in grey pencil (**a**).

2   Paint in the shapes of the heads with black fabric paint (**b**), and follow the manufacturer's instructions to set the paint.

3   Layer the quilt top with the wadding and backing, ensuring that there is an even border of the backing fabric outside the wadding and quilt top, then quilt as you wish by hand or machine (**c**).

4   Bring the background fabric to the front of the quilt in a double fold and stitch down the folded edge by hand or machine. (If you prefer, you can use a separate binding strip rather than bringing the backing over to create the binding.)

5   Stitch the beads on in pairs to create the eyes (**d**). You could make the eyes from french knots in white thread, instead of using beads.

a   b   c   d

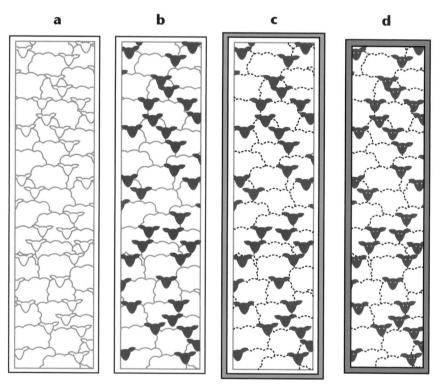

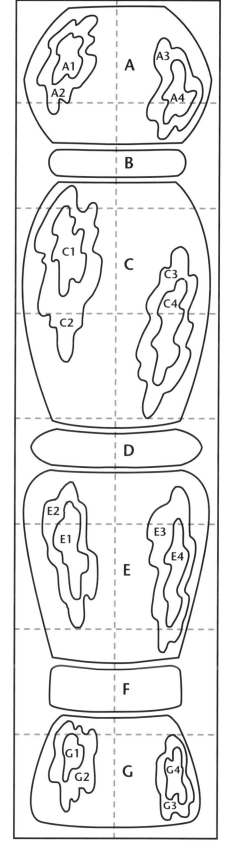

YOU WILL NEED:

- two 40 x 10in (1m x 25cm) pieces of black cotton fabric
- 40 x 10in (1m x 25cm) piece of flat wadding
- generous 1yd/1m bonding web
- four large pieces of silk dupion in bright colours for the pots, and patches of contrasting silks to create the dishes between the pots
- patches of toning silk dupions to go with each main pot colour – two lighter shades and two darker shades for each pot
- assorted green silks for the kawakawa leaves (I used three different greens), plus scraps of black fabric and scraps of wadding
- machine-stitching threads: black, plus colours to tone with your silks
- plain paper for enlarging the design, black felt pen, pencil, ruler

INSTRUCTIONS

1 Enlarge the quilt design as described on page 76. Lay the bonding web paper side up over the drawing and trace the shapes of the main pots and dishes in pencil. Then trace separately all the different shapes marking the highlights and the shadows. Mark all the traced shapes with their numbers, then cut them out roughly outside the marked lines.

2 Fuse the bonding web shapes onto the backs of the relevant fabrics, then cut the shapes out along the marked lines. Press one of the pieces of black fabric. Peel the backing papers off the pot and dish pieces, and position them on the black fabric in an even column, making sure that there's a border of black fabric between all the patches and at the top and bottom (**a**). Fuse the patches in place.

3 Remove the backing papers for the highlights and shadows of each pot and assemble them on the relevant shapes (the exact positions don't matter); fuse into place (**b**). Use toning thread to stitch random lines of machining across the highlight and shadow shapes to secure them.

4 Layer the quilt top with the wadding and backing, then work random lines of machining in black to and fro around all the cut edges of silk. Don't try and make them neat – they're supposed to be scruffy! (A walking foot is quite useful here.)

5 Cut around the entire column shape, leaving a more-or-less even border round the edge of each pot (**c**), then go over the cut edge with a small zigzag to seal it.

6 On the paper side of the remaining bonding web, draw some different-sized heart shapes (I made the largest one about 3in/7.5cm high and wide, and the smallest one about 1½in/4cm high and wide). Use the same technique to prepare, fuse, appliqué and stitch these patches onto black fabric scraps sandwiched with wadding, then cut them into rough heart shapes and seal the edges with zigzag (**d**).

7 Pin the largest kawakawa leaf to the bottom of the column and secure it with stitched veins fanning out from the top. Position the next leaf further up so that it overlaps and secure in the same way (**e**); continue with all the leaves, finishing with the smallest.

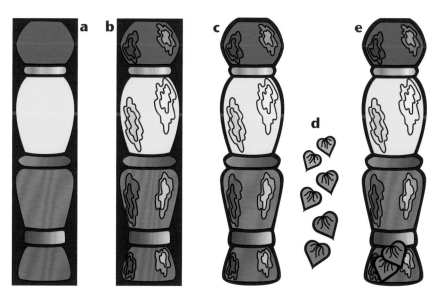

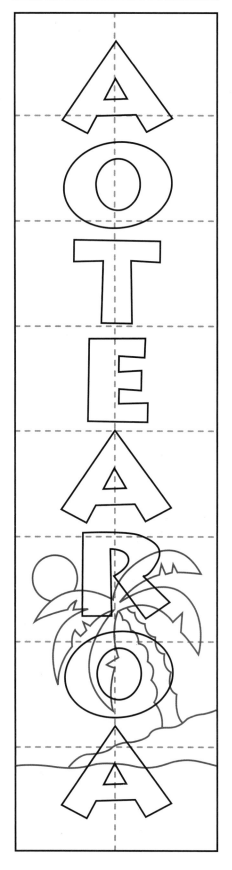

Aotearoa PATTERN

YOU WILL NEED:

- 40 x 10in (1m x 25cm) cloud-print cotton background fabric
- 40 x 10in (1m x 25cm) piece of firm white sheer fabric (choose a firm one so that it doesn't distort when you're assembling the design)
- 40 x 10in (1m x 25cm) piece of flat wadding
- 40 x 10in (1m x 25cm) piece of backing fabric
- quilting threads for your choice of hand or machine quilting
- 3yd (3m) binding (I used white satin binding, 1in/2.5cm wide)
- machine-stitching threads in pale blue, plus colours to match your island scene (greens, darker blue, brown, yellow)
- plain paper for enlarging the design, soft pencil, ruler and tracing (or greaseproof) paper
- patches of cotton fabrics in bright prints for the water, island, palm tree leaves and trunk, and sun
- two pieces of Stitch 'n' Tear or other tearaway foundation paper, one 40 x 7in (1m x 18cm) and one 12 x 10in (30 x 25cm)
- small, sharp-pointed scissors or appliqué scissors

INSTRUCTIONS

1 Enlarge the quilt design as described on page 76. Lay the sheer fabric right side up over the full-size drawing and trace the letters only in pencil (**a**).

2 Trace the shapes of the sun, palm leaves, trunk, island and water onto greaseproof paper. Cut these out and use them as templates to cut shapes from the relevant fabrics, using the templates right side up on the right sides of the fabrics. Pin the patches in position on the background (sky) fabric, starting with the sea and working upwards (**b**); overlap the patches slightly so that there are no gaps. Zigzag round the edges.

3 Pin the smaller piece of tearaway foundation under the island design, and work machine satin stitch (see p7) around the raw edges of the patches; begin with the sun, then work down through the trunk, palm leaves, island and finally the top of the sea. Once all the satin stitch is complete, tear away the foundation paper from the back of the design.

4 Lay the sheer fabric, right side up, over the design so that the raw edges align, and pin the layers together. Work a small machine zigzag around the edges of the letterforms, then use the small scissors to trim the sheer fabric carefully away from inside the letters, taking care not to cut the underneath fabric (**c**).

5 Layer the quilt top with the wadding and backing, then pin the larger piece of tearaway foundation paper behind the letters; work a line of pale blue machine satin stitch around the zigzagged edges of the letters (**d**). Tear the foundation paper away from the back of the work, then quilt the rest of the design as you wish by hand or machine. Bind the edges to complete the quilt.

a

b

c

d